"While this book may be designed for teaching young people (children), this is a treasure trove of fun, wisdom and action-packed activities for the entire family, from the youngest to the eldest.

What a wonderful collection of wisdom-driven inquiries and imagination-driven illustrations! Each "Tao" is a gem! A stand-alone jewel of guidance for every family open to learning and growing spiritually while having fun.

The questions we ask about life are what defines our quality of life and this collection is packed with seminal inquiry for any mind at any age of development.

The combination of story, wisdom, and action for each "Tao" is a brilliant teaching tool for the whole family.

I've been a family therapist and spiritual leader for three decades and wish I had had at my fingertips this delightful and delicious collection for myself and my family as well as for my congregants and clients. Well here it is now. Gobble it up with gusto and gratitude for the gift the authors and illustrator have given us all."

Sheila Pearl, MSW
Director, Mind-Body-Spirit Connections Life Coaching Programs
Co-author with Jack Canfield in "Pearls of Wisdom: 30 Inspirational Ideas...",
Author of "Still Life: A Spiritual Guidebook for Family Caregivers," and co-author with Arielle Ford in "Wake Up Women Be Happy, Healthy & Wealthy: A Guidebook by 50 Coaches"
www.SheilaPearl.com

"If you want to introduce the principles of the Tao to young children, I know of no better book than I Know the Way: 81 Fun Ways to live the Tao. In this heart and mind opening book by Nilanjana Krishnan and Bob Umlas, the Tao's timeless gems are expressed in age-appropriate, creative, and fun ways. The wisdom of each verse of the Tao is cracked open with stories, words of wisdom, engaging activities, reflection, and affirmations. Appealing to a diversity of children's learning styles, Nilanjana and Bob's book draws children in to want to learn and experience more. Though I Know the Way is geared to be read to children, adults will be drawn into this book's unique, fresh, and insightful approach to Lao Tzu's Tao TeChing."

Rev. Matthew Carriker
Protestant Chaplain, Brandeis University
Author of "Giving Christianity Back to Jesus"
www.backtojesusnow.com

I Know the Way

81 Fun Ways to Live the Tao

Authors
Nilanjana Krishnan
Bob Umlas

Illustrated By
Dhivya Kaliappan

Copyright © 2012 Nilanjana Krishnan
All rights reserved.
ISBN-10: 146639272X
EAN-13: 9781466392724
Library of Congress Control Number: 2011917850
CreateSpace Independent Publishing Platform
North Charleston, South Carolina

The authors of this book do not dispense medical advice or prescribe the use of any technique as a form of treatment for physical, emotional, or medical problems without the advice of a physician, either directly or indirectly. The intent of the authors is only to offer information of a general nature to help you in your quest for emotional and spiritual well-being. In the event you use any of the information in this book for yourself—as is your constitutional right—the authors assume no responsibility for your actions.

This book is dedicated to my precious children, Harsha and Rishab, and to every child in every family in every place in this world.

—*Nilanjana Krishnan*

I Acknowledge With Gratitude...

...Dr. Wayne Dyer, for his inspirational book, *Change your Thoughts, Change your Life—Living the Wisdom of the Tao*, which has served as our primary reference material.

...Neale Donald Walsch and the messages from his *Conversations with God* trilogy of books. They brought to life a latent potential inside me, and I began looking at myself and the world around me in a different way. Also, the Life Education Program offered by the CwG Foundation changed the course of my life forever by offering me tools to begin my "inward" journey.

...Linda Ratto, former director of the School of the New Spirituality and a wonderful lightworker, author, and leader, with whom I share the mission of advocating for our children, the leaders of tomorrow. She has been my teacher and inspiration and has helped me see how experiential learning, using lesson plans and activities, can enable our youngsters to realize the true essence of new spirituality principles.

...Bob Umlas and Dhivya Kaliappan, my team members, for contributing their wisdom toward co-creating this material with so much dedication and enthusiasm.

...Venky, my husband—whose presence served as a gentle wind beneath my sails—for his support and timely suggestions at those critical moments of the project.

...Harsha, my son, for offering wonderful ideas for some of the activities suggested in the book.

...family and friends, who have been instrumental in my journey and have contributed by speaking words of encouragement, showing faith and confidence in this message, offering feedback on the writing, and very often just by lending a listening ear or being witness to my chosen path.

...you, who are holding this material in your hands. Without you, this book would mean nothing.

Nilanjana Krishnan
Seattle, WA (USA)

I Acknowledge With Gratitude...

...Judy, my wife, for her unending support in my writing this book, for encouraging our both being on a spiritual journey in our lives, her support of my taking weekend days here and there to drive 150 miles to collaborate with my co-author on the content and concepts in the book, and for her unending love.

...Werner Erhard, creator of *est* and the Landmark Forum, and his staff, for opening me up in 1976 to being receptive to even the *idea* of spirituality! I was so closed to the idea prior to that time. I now live in an entirely different, satisfying world of possibility.

...Esther and Jerry Hicks, for opening me up further in the realm of spirituality, inspiring me to be more frequently and consistently in the presence of the divine and the Tao.

...Nilanjana Krishnan, my partner in writing this material, for her spirit, her support, her lightness of being, her dedication, her love.

Bob Umlas
Palisades, NY (USA)

Contents

Introduction		xv
A Note From Bob		xix
1.	The pathway to knowing anything is to let it be without labeling	1
2.	Things exist because their opposites exist	3
3.	Things have value only because of your desire for them	5
4.	The power that creates everything is invisible and always exists	9
5.	Appreciating all things equally allows for appreciating all things	11
6.	The invisible power that creates appears in various forms	13
7.	Serve the needs of others to have all your needs fulfilled	17
8.	Life is easier when we follow our nature	21
9.	Stop pouring when your cup is full, or a dozen would have thirteen	23
10.	Separation is an illusion, so see yourself in all	25
11.	Walls may create a room, but the usefulness is the empty space	29
12.	True mastery is not in possessing stuff but in trusting your inner vision	31
13.	Not high status but an independent mind makes life trouble-free	33
14.	That which is not understood easily may be known intuitively	37
15.	Be patient, calm, and watchful as the future unfolds	39
16.	Change is constant, so holding onto something is not useful	43
17.	Gravity invisibly and quietly sets the rules, and everyone learns	47
18.	No rules means no opposition, thereby creating the freedom to be	51
19.	Living with no attachment to outside approval is satisfying	55
20.	Go with the flow and accept what is in front of you	59
21.	To master the mysterious give up trying to figure it out	63
22.	Palm trees survive hurricanes because they yield to the force	65
23.	The nature of water allows it to take the shape of its container	69
24.	Excess of anything does not serve	71
25.	Viewing yourself as great makes you great	73
26.	See life as an adventure and appreciate all events with calmness	77

27.	A good person is good to the good and good to the bad	81
28.	Preserve your unique qualities and be an eternally powerful leader	85
29.	Life unfolds naturally and perfectly, with no need of control	87
30.	Using power for wrongful deeds weakens you	89
31.	True nature of man is peace	93
32.	Connect with the invisible power for perfect harmony	95
33.	Understanding oneself is wisdom	99
34.	Greatness is not achieved by domination	101
35.	Happiness is felt only when its presence within us is acknowledged	103
36.	To naturally flourish, do not try to get attention	107
37.	The world can transform itself using minimal efforts to change	111
38.	A person living his true nature is never aware of it	115
39.	You are a part of the whole	117
40.	Surrender to the invisible creator	121
41.	Appearances may be deceptive	123
42.	Come together as one and gain	125
43.	The truly powerful go about easily and effortlessly	130
44.	Give up the need for more, and know when to stop	131
45.	Not outward grandeur, but peace of mind is true accomplishment	135
46.	Heaven on Earth is guaranteed for the content at heart	139
47.	More can be accomplished by doing less and with less effort	141
48.	Accumulating less and letting go are true strengths	145
49.	Be kind, not self-righteous	149
50.	The immortal spirit enjoys a temporary human experience	151
51.	The unseen power guides and protects without possessing	153
52.	All of creation can trace its origin to the same eternal mother	157
53.	Honesty and compassion are divine qualities	161
54.	The power that creates the world is made visible in your good deeds	165
55.	Harmony and letting go endure, but not force and control	167
56.	You know best what to say and do	169
57.	Do not impose rules	171
58.	Life is a beautiful cycle of alternating good and bad fortunes	175
59.	Where there is moderation, there is no limit	179
60.	Avoid harming another, and all of life's benefits will flow to you	181
61.	One wins friendship and trust by surrendering and remaining still	183

Contents

62.	Forgive those who hurt you and accept everyone	185
63.	Simplify the complicated	189
64.	A journey of a thousand miles begins with one step	191
65.	Look within your heart for answers	195
66.	Humility is where real power lies	197
67.	Lead with mercy, frugality, and humility	199
68.	Good friends work as a team instead of competing	201
69.	When hostility exists, there is no room for love	205
70.	Practicing the simplicities of life brings true joy	209
71.	Awareness of the present moment removes all illnesses	213
72.	Admire and accept the perfect miracle that is you	217
73.	Live in grace, and trust that prayers are answered in perfect time	221
74.	All things here today are gone tomorrow	225
75.	Place fewer demands on yourself and others	229
76.	True power lies in being flexible at all times	231
77.	Abundance grows when excess is given away	233
78.	The soft and supple is often stronger than the rigid and hard	237
79.	Where there is harshness, extend kindness	239
80.	Paradise is appreciating life in the here and now	243
81.	Be good, do good; and give more, hoard less	245
References		249

Introduction

I am so grateful to your beautiful soul for being guided to this book. It's my dream—my earnest desire—that this material reaches your hands and serves as one of the tools to support you in your spiritual journey. If you were drawn to this book, it is highly likely that you have, by divine grace, been granted the privilege of raising or caring for at least one child, be it your own or someone else's. Congratulations!

As a mother of two boys (ages eight and three), I am constantly reading and researching material on how to relate better with my children. This journey has brought me the awareness that it's imperative for parents to heal their relationship with themselves before they can even hope to effectively and lovingly relate with their children. My inner quest thus led me on many paths to self-development, and one of them happened to be a book titled *Change Your Thoughts, Change Your Life—Living the Wisdom of the Tao,* written by Dr. Wayne Dyer. This book has changed the course of my life forever. The simple, yet profound teachings, so beautifully articulated, touched my soul very deeply. I heard a still, small voice say to me, "How about creating a children's version of this book?" Believe it or not, I actually jumped up from my seat, opened a Word document on my laptop computer, and penned down (sorry, keyed in) my initial thoughts on the subject. I could not ignore this deep calling. The energy was real and present in the room with me. I knew in my heart instantly that if I wanted my children to have a holistic view on life, then I must *be* the change first. Thus, was created *I Know the Way: 81 Fun Ways to Live the Tao*—my first concrete step in this journey of being the change I wish to see in my children (and all children of this planet). Can you think of a more fun way to experience wholeness and healing as a family than to experience it with your own children? This book is ideally suited for all those wonderfully nurturing relationships—parent and child; teacher and student; grandparent and grandchild; coach and trainee...you name it. I see families opening their homes and gathering as a community to experience the wisdom of the Tao along with their children through the format of playdates, circle time, study groups, book clubs, and so on. This book is also well-suited for individual reading.

As the name suggests, this book is based on the *Tao Te Ching*, an ancient Chinese philosophy authored by Lao Tzu. The word *Tao* means "the Way," *Te* means "virtue," and *Ching* means "great book." There are a total of eighty-one verses in the Tao, and they each serve in guiding us to be true to our own nature, simply by *being*. I suppose this is all it takes to be a human *being* (otherwise, our species would probably be referred to as "human doings"!).

I am so blessed to have been able to invite into my life some amazing people, whose contribution to this project has been *invaluable*. Bob Umlas, the co-author of this book, has contributed the "WoW" (Words of Wisdom) section. We met at the Landmark Forum, where I happened to tell him about this journey I was on and that I was eagerly looking for a likeminded person to support me in my book project. Bob mentioned that he had written several "Words of Wisdom" for his daughter, to teach her basic life lessons in a lighthearted way. As soon as I heard this, I felt the goose bumps (a nod from heaven). I asked if he would be interested in contributing WoWs for each of the eighty-one verses of the Tao and write them as if they were for his daughter. He agreed and came onboard! Next, our project required an illustrator for the fables. We went searching in all the unlikely places, but she was right before our eyes—Dhivya Kaliappan, my sweet and charming sister-in-law (my husband's sister), was so delighted by the project that she signed up to do the illustrations, using her own approach, well suited for both the young and the young at heart.

The layout of *I Know the Way: 81 Fun Ways to Live the Tao* is pretty self-explanatory. There are eighty-one chapters in all, one for each of the eighty-one verses. Every chapter has seven sections, which are presented in the following sequence:

1. A quotation, alluding to the verse.

2. An illustrated fable—adapted from Aesop's fables—directly or indirectly touching upon the verse, using humor or satire.

3. Words of Wisdom (WoW), a one-paragraph explanation of the verse using analogies, metaphors, and/or examples.

4. An activity, providing an experiential understanding of the Tao verse. Modifying the activity to suit your needs (as a family, group of families, or community) is encouraged, for what is practicable in America in December may not be in Australia or India. You get the idea, don't you? Adult supervision is essential, even when not specifically indicated within the activity.

5. Some questions for exploration as a follow-up to the activity. This could be arranged in any format you please and may even differ from time to time, depending on the number of participants. It is essential for an adult to be present as a facilitator to pose the questions and to ensure a safe, comfortable space for children to express themselves. You may also encourage the participants to record their thoughts and feelings in a journal.

6. Keywords to introduce some new, positive vocabulary as an expression of the Tao verse.

7. An affirmation for programming the subconscious mind to resonate with the Tao essence. This is a statement normally made in the first-person present tense; it is recommended that it be repeated several times a day for optimum results. Here again, it is encouraged that every individual devise his or her own best practices for doing the affirmations. One suggestion would be to repeat the affirmation three times by placing the right hand over the heart, feeling the energy generated by the statement.

You will find that the book speaks directly to the child, instructing him or her to be in control and own this experience. It has placed him or her in the driver's seat. Do you know what happens when a child is empowered? Magic happens. The magic is *your* healing. Trusting the child and letting go brings healing to the family, the community, the nation, the planet. Be there to guard and protect the child from physical harm or danger, but let go of controlling his or her dreams and desires.

I am on this journey with you. May this book support us in experiencing this magical healing and in renewing our relationship with the child (or children) in our lives.

Nilanjana Krishnan
Seattle, WA (USA)

A Note From Bob

Meeting Nilanjana Krishnan in September 2008 during my fifteenth (or so) Landmark Forum was a major turning point in my spiritual growth. In our first meeting, we discovered a lot about each other—that we had both been taken by the *Conversations with God* series of books, the materials by Abraham and Esther Hicks, an interest in Zen, and so on. She shared with me this project she was working on, and I found it very intriguing. I shared with her some of the things I had said to my daughter when she was a teenager, which meant a lot to her, and which I had called "Words of Wisdom." Nilanjana really liked what I said and asked if I'd like to write more of these to make her work become the Tao book you are holding in your hands. I hesitated, because I didn't know if I could do it, and I also was not all that familiar with the Tao. But I so connected with her spirit and energy, I simply couldn't say no. She asked me to read Wayne Dyer's book, *Change Your Thoughts, Change Your Life*, about his take on the eighty-one Tao verses, and write my words of wisdom to each one. I spent the next year or so doing that, meeting with Nilanjana every so often (at that time we lived a few hundred miles apart, and currently live a few thousand miles apart), and fine-tuning and reworking both of our writings.

I found being in her space inspiring and spiritual, and she found the same about me. We really connected and felt we shared a deep passion for this work. I feel like I got a lot smarter about life, people, and things. On January 1, 2009, I declared a shift in being regarding food (I was about forty pounds overweight). I didn't change anything, I didn't go on a diet—I shifted who I was. I simply became a person who never had an issue with food. I attribute this totally to being on this spiritual adventure with Nilanjana. I lost about twenty-eight pounds, literally without doing anything.

I found that being in this process was somewhat self-fulfilling and self-propelling. That is, just by declaring it, it happened; it manifested; it became alive. It was the adventure of a lifetime. Thankfully, I had the full support of my wife, who also benefited from my becoming what she refers to as "Buddha Bob"—the me without opinions, without history; the me that evolved by being so connected to the Tao, the essential truth about things. Again, this is all attributed to my connection to the work Nilanjana and I did together. I feel privileged to be able to co-write this book with her and to share it with you all.

I

The pathway to knowing anything is to let it be without labeling

"A rose by any other name would smell as sweet."
—WILLIAM SHAKESPEARE

The Cat-Maiden

Once upon a time, high up in the beautiful blue skies, Jupiter and Venus were having a conversation about whether the nature of a person could ever change. Jupiter said, "Yes, the nature of a person can change," but Venus said, "No, the nature of a person can never change." The two decided to test it for themselves. So they chose a cat, turned her into a young lady, and gave her as a bride to a young gentleman. At the wedding, Jupiter observed how well this young lady behaved. He called to Venus and said, "Look, she is nothing like the cat she once was. She is a refined young lady." To this Venus replied, "Just wait a minute," and let loose a mouse into the room. As soon as the young lady spotted the mouse, she jumped, then pounced on the unsuspecting mouse. To this, both Venus and Jupiter remarked, "Ah, this cat is both ladylike and catlike!"

WoW: You see a beautiful flower. You smell it, and you love it. You ask someone, "What is it?" They say, "It's a tulip." You say, "A tulip? It's not like what I thought a tulip was!" Now you've destroyed the beautiful flower. It was beautiful before you gave it the label, but now it's a not-tulip; a wrong-tulip; a less-than-tulip. By labeling the beauty, the beauty became less. You added a description to the flower. The flower was whole and complete by itself, without your description! When you add to something that's complete, you take away from its original wholeness. To understand a flower is to let it be, without giving it a label.

Activity: Create a flower or kitchen garden with your family and friends. Make sure to pick the seeds with your eyes shut, or have an adult strike out the name from the seed packets. Now, lovingly sow and water them. Notice the seedlings, buds, and leaves that slowly start appearing. Appreciate how, by simply *allowing*, the beautiful garden you imagined is created.

Explore: Can you identify what flower, vegetable, or fruit is growing in your garden? How do you think they got their names? Would these wondrous creations somehow be different if we called them by any name other than the one we are familiar with?

Keywords: Noninterference, nonlabeling

Affirmation: I allow everything just as nature intends.

2

Things exist because their opposites exist

"I have found the paradox that if I love until it hurts, then there is no hurt, but only more love."

—MOTHER TERESA

The Man and His Two Wives

In a small town called Toovania, there lived a man with two wives. One wife was much younger than he, and the other was much older. The young wife was upset and cried, "My husband looks so old, people will think he is my father." The old wife in turn wailed, "My husband looks so young, people will think he is my son." So the two wives decided to do something to fix it. When the man was fast asleep, the young wife plucked out all his gray hairs, and the old wife plucked out all his dark hairs. The next morning, when the man woke up and looked in the mirror, guess what he saw? A bald man!

WoW: If you watch someone looking down the street, saying, "No car, no car, no car..." what do you expect to eventually see? A car, of course. Hearing someone say "no car" makes you think of "car." The notion of "no tree" brings up the idea of "tree." One defines the other. You can't have the back of a hand without a front of the hand. Imagine this (this is not easy): what completely surrounds a tree is "no tree." Imagine removing the tree but leaving the "no tree." What's in the space where the tree was? If you're leaving the "no tree," there *must* be tree in that space. One simply cannot exist without the other. Without the description, things are whole.

Activity: Get together with friends and, with the help of an adult, play any game that you like, with the condition that whoever *plays* the game will be declared a winner.

Explore: How did it feel to share your success with others? How differently did you experience this game? Could you tell who lost the game and how? Would you enjoy any activity if there were no winners or losers declared at the end? Why or why not?

Keywords: Acceptance, effortlessness, oneness

Affirmation: I choose to enjoy any game, no matter the outcome.

3

Things have value only because of your desire for them

"The most valuable things in life are not measured in monetary terms. The really important things are not houses and lands, stocks and bonds, automobiles and real estate, but friendships, trust, confidence, empathy, mercy, love and faith."

—BERTRAND RUSSELL

The Miser and His Gold

Once upon a time, there lived a man who used to hide all his gold coins at the foot of a small tree in his garden. Every week, he would go to the tree, dig up his gold, and take pride in his wealth. There was a robber who noticed these weekly visits by the man, and one day he went stealthily into the garden himself, dug up all the gold, and stole it. When the man returned to his garden to gloat over his wealth, he was shocked and cried, "All my wealth is gone. What will I do now? How will I ever live without it?" Hearing his cries, a neighbor came up to him and asked, "Do you ever take any of your gold out?" To this the man responded, "No, I don't. I simply come to look at it every week." To this the neighbor responded, "Don't take it to heart, my friend; put a brick in the hole, and look at it every day—it will be as useful to you as your gold."

WoW: Why do you buy things for yourself? So you can have them, of course. Once you have them, there's some initial excitement at the newness of what it is you now have, and you enjoy playing with it or looking at it, but after a short time, the desire to buy or have something else seems to come along, and you then desire the *next* thing. If you notice your friend buying something "cool," you may also notice that you want to have something at *least* as cool if not better, so now you want something new, and this process continues. What you may eventually notice is that the thing you're getting is *not* the thing that brings you contentment, and it's also not the *process* of getting things that brings you contentment. The search for contentment has the idea "I'm not content" built into the search, because if you *were* content, you would not be looking for it! Contentment comes from simply *being* satisfied with what you have, and if something new comes along, being content with *that*.

Activity: Get together with your friends and play only with empty cardboard boxes, packages, cartons, and/or old-fashioned, "traditional" toys. Avoid playing with the latest automated, computer-based, battery-operated, or remote-controlled toys.

Explore: Did you enjoy playing with these simple toys? Did you miss your "other," regular toys? How different was your experience playing with these new toys? Do you think one must have expensive toys to feel happy? If so, why?

Keywords: Minimize, surrender, selflessness

Affirmation: I value serving others more than gathering stuff.

4

The power that creates everything is invisible and always exists

"Ninety-nine percent of who you are is invisible and untouchable."
—RICHARD BUCKMINSTER FULLER

The Boy and the Man

It was a very cold winter night. A boy who was roaming the woods lost his way and was spotted by an elderly man who lived nearby. As it was getting dark, this elderly man offered to help the boy and took him to his house for the night, saying that he would guide him out of the forest in the morning. While they were walking to the man's house, the boy felt really cold. So he cupped both his hands, raised them to his mouth, and started blowing on them. "What do you do that for?" asked the man. "My hands are numb with the cold," said the boy, "and my breath warms them." "Oh, I see," said the man. After they went inside the house, the man poured hot soup into a bowl for the boy to eat. When the boy raised his spoon to his mouth he began blowing upon it. "And what do you do that for?" asked the elderly man. "The soup is too hot, and my breath will cool it," said the boy. "How is that?" asked the man. "Both hot and cold with the same breath?" The boy responded, "That's because you don't see the power that enables me to make my breath hot or cold, as and when I desire."

WoW: The Tao is the built-in nature of things, the nature of being, the nature of God. The Tao doesn't exist as a "thing," and yet it's always present. It isn't any stuff, any being, or God. It may be like water to a fish—the fish doesn't know about the water; it's the nature of the water that allows for fish. It's the nature of air that allows for birds. The Tao allows for you. And the Tao always exists; therefore, so do *you*!

Activity: Play the "pretending" game with friends. Pretend that you *are* something (say, a dinosaur, a doctor, an astronomer, or whatever), or take any prop or material and play "make-believe" (example: make believe you have a car, spaceship, robot, etc.). Experience the joy of being and/or having it now, even when you know that it is unreal.

Explore: Did you miss *being* the "thing" or *having* the "thing"? What do you think made the experience "real" for you? What held your interest in this game?

Keywords: Limitlessness, possibilities, accessibility

Affirmation: I can be, do, and have whatever I humbly desire.

5
Appreciating all things equally allows for appreciating all things

"The good we secure for ourselves is precarious and uncertain until it is secured for all of us and incorporated into our common life."

—Jane Addams

The Birds, the Beasts, and the Bat

In a jungle somewhere in Asia, a group of birds were having a fight with a group of beasts. Among these birds and beasts was a bat that thought, "If I stay with the winning group, then I can declare myself a winner. Yeah!" Thinking this thought, the bat kept shuttling between the two groups, depending on who was appearing to win. Finally, both the birds and the beasts got tired of fighting and decided to make peace with each other. Once peace was restored, neither the birds nor the beasts wanted anything to do with the bat.

WoW: When you are whole, there is no "taking sides." When you are whole, lacking nothing, you have room for all things to exist. If you focus on a particular thing, you've all of a sudden taken sides; you've made the thing "special." You bring the thing's specialness into existence by your focus on it. Talking about it is focusing on it. Making it special is focusing on it. You don't need to focus on it. Let it be, and enjoy its wholeness.

Activity: Make a list of some or all of your favorite items at home. Now, give away one of those items to someone whom you do not know from before (perhaps through the Salvation Army or another charitable organization).

Explore: How does it feel to give away something you love? Do you consider yourself special for being able to give? Is the one who receives your gift special? What makes someone special? Can every person be special? Why or why not?

Keywords: Harmony, sharing

Affirmation: Each life on Earth is as precious as mine.

6

The invisible power that creates appears in various forms

"While I know myself as a creation of God, I am also obligated to realize and remember that everyone else and everything else are also God's creation."

—MAYA ANGELOU

The Girl and the Wolf

A young girl, returning home alone from a nearby field, was being followed by a wolf. Seeing she could not escape, she turned around, and said: "I know, friend wolf, that I must be your prey, but before you eat me, I ask for just one favor." The wolf agreed, and the girl continued, "Would you please play me a tune to which I may dance?" The wolf complied, and while he was playing the tune and the girl was dancing, some hounds hearing the sound ran up and began chasing the wolf. Turning to the girl, he said, "It is just what I deserve; I should not have turned a musician to please you." The girl said to herself, "Thank you, Gods and Angels, for helping me create this brilliant idea that helped save my life."

WoW: The Tao is empty, meaning it contains no "stuff." It just *is*. It is the condition where everything is possible, so it gives birth to more possibility. So it's like a mother in that it gives birth. You have that inside you; it is who you are—possibility/everything. If you say "I don't cry," then you've limited yourself, because now you can't. You've made yourself be someone who can't cry, and to cry would make "yourself" wrong. If you say, "Who I am is happy," you limit yourself in the same way: if you found yourself being sad, then the way you just described yourself is no longer valid. Instead, don't describe yourself as a particular way—describe yourself as all ways, or no way. Now you have the ability or room to be all. You can create yourself to be anything. Nothing will make you wrong. Nothing will make your ideas wrong. This is the Tao.

Activity: Get together with friends and place a variety of different toys or games inside a box. Now each of you draws out one toy or game from here, and you each help someone who has a toy or game that *you* are most skilled in operating or playing with. You also allow someone who has talent in using your toy or game to assist you.

Explore: How did it feel to be able to lend your talent to someone? Did you enjoy learning new things in this creative way? Were you able to express yourself while helping your friend? Could your receiving the assistance been a gift for your friend?

Keywords: Inspiration, uniqueness, co-creation

Affirmation: I graciously receive all the good that comes my way.

7

Serve the needs of others to have all your needs fulfilled

"We are formed and molded by our thoughts. Those whose minds are shaped by selfless thoughts give joy when they speak or act. Joy follows them like a shadow that never leaves them."

—Buddha

The Donkey and the Mule

A man started out on a journey, driving before him a donkey and a mule, both well laden. As long as the donkey traveled along plain roads, he could carry his load with ease, but when he began to climb the steep path of the mountain, he felt his load to be more than he could bear. He requested his companion, the mule, to help him with a small portion of the load, so that he might carry home the rest; but the mule paid no attention to the request. The donkey soon fell down dead under the burden. The man could not figure out what to do in such a wild mountainous region; so he placed upon the mule the load that the donkey had been carrying as well as the hide of the dead donkey. The mule groaned and sighed at the load he had to now carry and said to himself: "If I had only assisted the donkey in his time of need, I would now not be carrying this entire load all by myself."

WoW: Imagine a group of men who, each night before bedtime, put their shoes outside their doors because the custom of the place was that any shoes placed outside the door would be shined (or polished) for the next morning. Now imagine that one morning, everyone discovered their shoes were stolen. Most likely, they would be angry at the thieves! Imagine if one man considered that his shoes were *not* stolen, but merely borrowed, and he was the one chosen to fulfill the wish of another, more needy person. Then he would feel good, while everyone else would feel bad. When you give up pretending that things belong to you, then you are freer to enjoy all things. After all, is that tree-house really *yours*? Isn't it just an arrangement of pieces of wood, coming from and belonging to *Nature*?

Activity: Arrange a potluck lunch, dinner, or snack time get-together with your friends. Invite each person to bring one dish to share with the group. Appreciate how you get to enjoy many different types of treats when you only contributed one item to the spread.

Explore: Would it have been easier or more difficult if you had the responsibility of bringing all of the food? How did it feel to both contribute and receive? Did you enjoy being able to accomplish and experience much more this way? If so, how?

Keywords: Allowing, vulnerability, service

Affirmation: I am joyfully available for anyone in need.

8

Life is easier when we follow our nature

"Adopt the pace of nature: her secret is patience."
—RALPH WALDO EMERSON

The Goose with the Golden Eggs

One day a farmer went to the nest of his goose and found there an egg, all yellow and glittering. When he picked up the egg, it seemed very heavy. The farmer thought that he had been tricked. On second thought, however, he took the egg home; and to his sheer delight, he discovered that the egg was of pure gold. To his utter amazement, the same thing happened each day after that: the goose would lay a golden egg; he would take the egg to the market, sell it, and make a lot of money. As the farmer grew richer and richer day after day, he started becoming greedy. So he decided to kill the goose to collect all the golden eggs at once. But when he killed the goose and cut her open, he found nothing inside.

WoW: One of the benefits of water is that it nourishes life. It does so by *doing* nothing—rather, it does it by simply *being* water. If you threw a stone into the water, it would still "be" water that nourishes life. One of the benefits of *you* is probably unconditional love (or being helpful, punctual, etc.), and this benefit requires you to *do* absolutely nothing. It's your nature. That's real being. When you simply "be," there is nothing to do; there is nothing to have. Being involves doing nothing. Doing whatever you're doing, without letting the chatter in your head bother you—just as the stone does not bother the water—is "being." Be like water. Go with the flow.

Activity: Get together with friends and, with the assistance of an adult, make your own cheese (cottage cheese or Indian paneer cheese) by following the instructions in a recipe book. Or you may use the recipe on this website link: http://showmethecurry.com/odds-ends/homemade-paneer-indian-cheese.html. Enjoy the step by step process. Pay attention to how each step in the process clearly indicates when to begin the next step (example: the boiling milk indicates that the lemon juice must be added, etc.).

Explore: Did you enjoy the process of creating? Were you patiently waiting for guidance, or were you getting impatient? Did you realize how the process itself revealed the next steps without you making any effort? In what other ways is life similar to this experience in the kitchen?

Keywords: Freedom, authenticity, rhythmic

Affirmation: I feel wonderful expressing my true feelings.

9

Stop pouring when your cup is full, or a dozen would have thirteen

"There is a sufficiency in the world for man's need but not for man's greed."
—MOHANDAS GANDHI

The Dog and the Reflection

One day, a dog who had found a bone was taking it home to eat it in peace. On her way home, she had to cross a plank lying across a running brook. As she was crossing the stream, she looked down and saw her reflection in the water below. Thinking it was another dog with another bone, she thought, "I want that bone also!" As soon as the dog opened her mouth to snap at the "other dog," which was nothing but her own reflection, the bone she was holding in her mouth dropped into the water and was lost forever.

WoW: Imagine being at the beach and playing with the sand. You get a pail and start making some structure with the packed wet sand in the pail. You make this the foundation of your magnificent structure. You keep piling up more and more little pails of your building and have something big and beautiful, and you're proud of it. Now you get even more pails of sand, but the building can no longer withstand the weight of all the sand. It all comes crumbling down, and you're left with just a pile of sand, not the beautiful thing you just built. Now imagine something else similar: did you ever try to build a house of playing cards? Careful placement of the cards allows for a tall but fragile structure. Once again, too many cards, and it all comes crashing down. Life is sometimes like that. You're building something out of your life, but you may forget to stop and enjoy what you've built. Be careful—it may also come crashing down!

Activity: Go into your storage room or garage and make a list of the items (such as toys, clothes, books, etc.) you haven't used in a long time.

Explore: Do you still require them? Do you love them? Do these items evoke the same feelings of excitement as when you first got them? What does the phrase "enough is enough" mean to you? In what other areas of your life have you experienced that "enough is enough"?

Keywords: Moderation, sufficiency, satisfaction

Affirmation: I am happy with what I have.

10

Separation is an illusion, so see yourself in all

"There is no tree whose branches are foolish enough to fight amongst themselves."

—Native American Wisdom

The Kingdom of the Lion

A lion was preparing to take over as king of the jungle when he had a very rare dream. In his dream, he saw that the wolf and the lamb, the tiger and the stag, the leopard and the kid, and the dog and the hare all dwelt side by side in unbroken peace and friendship. When the lion woke up from his unusual dream, he called a meeting of all the beasts in the jungle, and announced, "Under the new code of laws, every animal shall live in perfect equality and harmony with every other animal in this jungle." Hearing this, the hare said, "Oh! How I have longed for this day, when the weak take their place without fear by the side of the strong!" All the other animals heartily agreed!

WoW: Did you ever notice that, no matter how nice someone is (say, a teacher), there will be someone who will not like him? Where does this likeable quality live—in the person or in you? Think of the president or prime minister of your country. There are those who like this person and those who don't. Where is this likeable quality—in the person or in you? Perhaps someone says something you think is brilliant, and someone else will say, "That's dumb." Which is it? It's all in the receiver or observer. There is nothing brilliant in what's said; there is no nice teacher, nor a likeable president or prime minister. You are the creator of it all—the brilliance or dumbness, niceness or badness, and likeable or unlikeable qualities. There's no separation between you and this other person. From what he or she does or says, you get to create an interpretation. This interpretation wouldn't even exist without the other person. You are connected, whether or not you agree with him or her. You're in an invisible partnership for the moment. There's no separation. You can love people and not impose your will, because you can love them as they are.

Activity: Invent a fun game where you pair up with a friend and introduce yourself to him or her by stating your partner's name; and he or she does the same (i.e., says your name when introducing himself or herself to you). Experience a sense of camaraderie and closeness.

Explore: If *your* name is [partner's name], what might you feel if someone pinched your arm or spoke harshly to you? How do you think your friend (having your name) might feel if he or she was treated the same way? Would your friend feel what you felt? Do you sense a feeling of oneness with your friend? Can you sense the same feeling of unity with others in your group and outside? If so, how?

Keywords: Inclusion, liberating, union

Affirmation: You and I are one.

II

Walls may create a room, but the usefulness is the empty space

"We cannot let another person into our hearts or minds unless we empty ourselves. We can truly listen to him or truly hear her only out of emptiness."

—M. Scott Peck

The Olive Tree and the Fig Tree

It was autumn, and the fig tree was losing all her leaves. An olive tree noticed the leaves falling and teased the fig tree, saying, "You lose your leaves every autumn and are bare till the spring, whereas I remain green all year round." Soon afterward, there came a heavy fall of snow, which settled on the leaves of the olive tree. The weight of the snow was so much that it bent and broke the olive tree, but the flakes fell harmlessly through the bare branches of the fig tree. The fig tree lived to bear many more crops.

WoW: If you were asked to point to yourself (go ahead, do it), you'd probably find that you're pointing to your heart. But is that where you are? If we were to cut you open, would we find you? Are you in there? Maybe who you are is not that. Maybe you're not even limited to your body. If someone broke your favorite toy, you'd be upset. Well, then, clearly you're not limited to your body, or something outside your body getting broken wouldn't upset you! So maybe who you are extends way beyond your body. Maybe across the street to your mom's car! If someone broke the car's window, you (and your mom!) would get upset. So you probably extend out everywhere and are not who you think. You're much bigger. So if who you are is *not* your body, maybe who you are is the space that you experience. A cereal bowl isn't only the material it's made out of; the space inside the bowl is what makes it useful. It's the "what is not" that helps to define the "what is."

Activity: Take any musical instrument. Play a single note for about ten to fifteen seconds. Now play different notes for a few seconds or perhaps a song you know. Observe how each note sounds to you and others.

Explore: Which did you and others enjoy listening to, the single or multiple notes? What was the difference between the two types of music you played? Did you notice the silence or gap between two notes? Can you make melodious music without these small gaps or intervals? Why or why not?

Keywords: Silence, innateness

Affirmation: I use the language of silence to imagine and create.

12

True mastery is not in possessing stuff but in trusting your inner vision

"You can never get enough of what you don't need to make you happy."

—Eric Hoffer

The Fox and the Crow

A fox once saw a crow fly off with a piece of cheese in its beak and settle on the branch of a tree. The fox thought, "That cheese is for me." So he walked up to the foot of the tree and said to the crow, "How beautiful you look today! Your feathers are so silky; your eyes are so bright. I am sure your voice must be wonderful, better than any other bird's." The crow was flattered at hearing the praise. Seeing this, the fox went on, "Let me hear one song from you, so I may call you 'Queen of the birds'." The crow lifted up her head and started to caw her best, but the moment she opened her mouth, the cheese fell to the ground. At once, the fox snapped up the cheese and ran away with it.

WoW: To be a master is to observe and allow. If you look for something beyond what is there, you destroy it, because you're no longer just observing it. Now you've added your personal wants to it. It's no longer pure. If you notice the color of some object, you've picked out something more than the whole object—you've added what you think is special about it. Although there *is* color, focusing on the color lessens the image's wholeness, as there's now focus, not wholeness. You know it's you doing the seeing, so you're creating what's out there. What you see and know outside of yourself comes from what's inside you. You can choose to see the whole or the parts. You can choose to see the beauty or not. Trust yourself.

Activity: Make a trip to a farm, or observe the trees or garden near your house. Savor the miracles of creation. Focus on *how* something is growing rather than *what* is growing. You may also visit a bakery to see *how* bread is made from different grains.

Explore: Were you fascinated at how something could grow or be made like this? What aspects did you find miraculous or enchanting? Would it have been equally fascinating if you had seen the farm as a picture in a book? Would you prefer to see water inside a plastic cup or water flowing in a stream? What holds your fascination more? Why? In what other areas of your life do you appreciate natural beauty?

Keywords: Curiosity, veneration

Affirmation: I see beauty in myself and in everyone around me.

13

Not high status but an independent mind makes life trouble-free

"You see things; and you say 'Why?' But I dream things that never were; and I say 'Why not?'"

—GEORGE BERNARD SHAW

The Man, the Boy, and the Donkey

A man and his son were taking their donkey with them to the market. Seeing the man and his son walk alongside the donkey, an onlooker remarked, "You have a donkey, and nobody's riding it?" Hearing this, the man put his son on the donkey, and they continued their journey. Soon they passed a group of people, one of whom said, "See that lazy boy; he lets his father walk while he rides." So the man ordered his son to get off and seated himself on the donkey's back. They hadn't gone far when they saw two women, one of whom said to the other, "Shame on that big man for letting his little boy walk." The man did not know what to do, so he placed the boy in front of him on the donkey's back and resumed the journey. By this time, they had reached the market, and the passersby began to criticize the man, saying, "Aren't you ashamed of yourself for burdening that poor donkey with the combined weight of you and your son?" The man and boy got off and tried to think what to do. They thought and thought, till at last they cut down a pole, tied the donkey's feet to it, and raised the pole and the donkey to their shoulders. They walked along and passed people who laughed at the sight. When they reached a bridge, the donkey got one of its feet loose, kicked out, and caused the boy to drop his end of the pole. In the struggle, the donkey fell over the bridge and into the water. "That will teach you to think for yourselves," said an old man, who had been following them.

WoW: Imagine people put you down—they say, "You're stupid." Do you know what they've really told you? They told you something about *themselves*! They told you that *they* think you're stupid. What does that have to do with *you*? Nothing. Now imagine people say to you, "You're great!" It's the same thing—they told you about *themselves*! Now imagine there's a CD left alone on the street inside a CD player, playing the voice of someone saying, "You're ugly" over and over—the entire content of the CD is this. If you walked by it, you wouldn't think it was really giving you disapproval. Yet we give people this power over us, needlessly. You don't need anyone's approval or disapproval to know yourself. Who you are is already whole and complete. Now go contribute *that* to others. Appreciate others for sharing themselves with you. There's nothing personal in what people say, just as there's nothing personal in that CD's message.

Activity: What would you like to be today? Get together with your friends and choose what you wish to be—a doctor, a chef, a mechanic, a race car driver, a nurse, etc. Become *that* for the day; think, speak, and act as if you are *that*. A few friends (or an adult facilitator) will sometimes deliberately criticize and at other times praise you on your chosen "profession." Simply notice how you feel when encouraged and when discouraged.

Explore: What did you enjoy about this activity? How did you feel when you were criticized or put down? How did you feel when you received praise? Did you feel like changing your chosen role based on what someone said? Why or why not?

Keywords: Self-expression, boundlessness

Affirmation: I listen to my inner voice and know what is best for me.

14

That which is not understood easily may be known intuitively

"I was always looking outside myself for strength and confidence, but it comes from within. It is there all the time."

—Anna Freud

The Peacock and the Crane

A peacock was teasing a crane about her dull and uninteresting feathers, saying, "Look at my brilliant colors; how bright and beautiful they look when compared to your poor feathers." "I agree with you," replied the crane, "but what you don't see is that when flying, I can soar into the clouds, whereas you are confined to the Earth like any plain chicken."

WoW: Did you ever want to be like someone else? Maybe you wanted to be able to fly like Superman. Maybe you wished you could trade places with someone else, at least for a while. Of course, you noticed also, that you *can't* fly like Superman or trade places with anyone else! That's probably a good thing, because someone *else* might want to trade places with *you*, and then where would *you* be? Who you are is someone with qualities and abilities that nobody else has, and true happiness and satisfaction lies in being content with what you already have. You don't need to look outside yourself for what's already inside!

Activity: Play the "blindfold game" with your friends. You may choose to use a large picture or poster of an animal (example: elephant) and draw its tail with blindfolded eyes based upon verbal cues from a friend. The cues may include stating the words, "cold," "warm," or "hot," depending upon how far or close you are to the spot where the tail should be drawn. Enjoy the accuracy (or inaccuracy) of your drawing. You and your friends could take turns drawing and giving directions. Next, try drawing an entire picture of something, blindfolded and without any verbal cues.

Explore: Can you describe what guided you to choose the spot to start the drawing (both the tail and the entire picture)? Which was easier, drawing the tail with verbal cues or drawing an entire picture without any verbal directions? No matter which was easier to draw, did you have fun playing this game? Is it always necessary to see, hear, or touch something to know or enjoy it? Why?

Keywords: Perception, eternal, mystical

Affirmation: I trust my intuition.

15

Be patient, calm, and watchful as the future unfolds

"It is the stillness that will save and transform the world."

—Eckhart Tolle

The Old Swallow and the Young Birds

An old swallow, watching a farmer sowing hemp seeds in a field, immediately told the young birds what the farmer was about. He knew that hemp was the material from which nets used in catching birds was made and advised them to join together in picking up the seeds before they took deep root. The birds neglected his advice. In a few days, the hemp appeared above the ground. The friendly swallow again patiently told them to remove the hemp, as he clearly saw what the future held for the birds if they didn't act quickly. The young birds again dodged his advice. So the old swallow chose not to argue; he left that area for his own safety and made his residence in a new, safe place. One day, as he was skimming along the streets, he happened to see many of these birds, imprisoned in a cage, on the shoulders of a bird-catcher.

WoW: Relax. Take a deep breath. Want what you actually have—physical things, time, or ideas—not what you think you should have. There's a famous saying: "All things come to those who wait." There's another: "Slow and steady wins the race." The next thing will come; it always does. Appreciate *that*. In your calmness, you can appreciate the now as well as the future. If you're waiting for what *you* want, you will frequently be disappointed, because it may not come. Give up that waiting, and the anxiety will disappear. The next *now* will show up. Look into the moment and whatever it contains—*there's* the adventure of life

Activity: Play the game of Hopscotch, where you draw rectangular box shapes in a specified pattern on the floor or ground and hop from box to box, ensuring that your feet do not touch the edges of the boxes. Enjoy this fun balancing act. See what happens when you play this game somewhat modified, with box shapes slightly smaller in size. Also see what happens if the boxes are numbered randomly, and you need to jump in sequence.

Explore: Was it easy playing this game? What made it possible for you to be able to balance? What might have happened had you hurried up and tried to finish the hops? Were you more mindful playing this game when slightly modified? If so, how? Do you think it pays to be alert, yet still?

Keywords: Patience, alertness, stillness

Affirmation: My calmness gives me the ability and readiness to face any situation.

16
Change is constant, so holding onto something is not useful

"When one door of happiness closes, another opens; but often we look so long at the closed door that we do not see the one which has been opened for us."

—Helen Keller

The Town Mouse and the Country Mouse

One day, a town mouse went to visit his cousin in the country. The country mouse welcomed his cousin and offered him beans, bacon, cheese, and bread. The town mouse was rather shocked and said, "Is this how you live and eat in the country? Come with me to my town, and I'll show you how to live." The country mouse agreed and went with his cousin on a visit to the town. They arrived at the town mouse's house pretty late at night, so the mouse took his cousin to get some food in the grand dining room. The country mouse saw the fare on the table and remarked, "Wow! Jellies, cakes, and ale! Yum!" The two had just started eating this grand feast, when they heard growling and barking. "What is that?" asked the country mouse. "It is only the dogs of the house," said the town mouse. "Only!" said the country mouse. Just then the door flew open, and in came two huge mastiffs. The two mice ran away for safety. "Good-bye, Cousin," said the country mouse. "What! Going so soon?" said the other. "Yes," he replied. "Better beans and bacon in peace than cakes and ale in fear." In his heart of hearts, the country mouse was glad that he got a taste of the grand feast without ever having to be bound to the town.

WoW: People often think of an end of something as a loss, or even a death, when really it's always a beginning and a birth! Imagine you're at a friend's house, having a really great time, and then you're told that you need to go home. You might be sad at the end of the great time, but only if you are focusing on that. If you're in the moment, noticing what's happening, you could see many new and wondrous things. For example, when you leave the house, maybe you see a beautiful sky, or huge trees, or perhaps some dogs romping across the street. And then you get home and a delicious dinner awaits. If you're focusing on your friend, your dinner won't taste very good. If you're aware of the beginning of your meal, you can enjoy every piece, being with your family—it's simply a new adventure. All of life is an adventure, and all particular adventures end only to reveal the *next* adventure. Whether it's exciting or sad is up to you.

Activity: Invent a game where you and your friends notice how endings become beginnings. Devote an entire day to a variety of different activities (such as playing, cooking, reading, discussing, napping, etc.) with the help of an adult facilitator. As you begin an activity, state the name of the activity and then say out loud, "This too shall pass!" and when you complete that activity, say aloud, "Welcome the new!" Celebrate this constancy of change.

Explore: Did you enjoy this experience of deliberately observing the cycle of changes? Did you miss anything in particular due to the temporary nature of each activity? What was the factor that was unchanging?

Keywords: Change, newness, unknown

Affirmation: I gladly welcome change.

17

Gravity invisibly and quietly sets the rules, and everyone learns

"If your actions inspire others to dream more, learn more, do more and become more, you are a leader."

—J̇OHN QUINCY ADAMS

The Frogs Asking for a King

A group of frogs were very eager to find a king who would rule over them. So they went to Jupiter and asked that he bring them a king. So Jupiter threw a log into their pool and said, "Here, welcome your king." The log made a loud splashing noise in the pool, which scared the frogs away. "The log is not moving at all," remarked one of the frogs. Another added, "What use is a king who lies in a pool of water and does not move?" So the frogs went back to Jupiter and requested that he take the log back and send them a new king instead. Jupiter removed the log and sent them a stork for a king. The stork began to catch the frogs and eat them, one by one.

WoW: Imagine the master is actually God (she is). Your everyday life is full of the nonawareness of her. She doesn't talk; she acts. When something is finished, you say you did it. What you should know is that you are God. You're usually not aware of your own existence—you're just doing what you're doing. And it is amazing…you did do it by yourself! When you do what you love to do, you're so involved in the doing that your enthusiasm will get others caught up in your project (or game), and the project will get done so much more quickly. It's not because you asked for help; your inner being called the universe's energy to line up with your project and called other beings or friends into alignment. Having this happen seemingly by accident is how an enlightened leader makes things happen. We all have that in us.

Activity: Choose one area in your environment, community, or family where you wish to make a change or improvement (example: recycling, sharing resources within the neighborhood, etc.). Be the change you want to effect (for instance, start recycling in your own room or house first, offer your vacuum cleaner or shovel to a friend or neighbor so that he or she need not buy one, and so on).

Explore: How was the experience of leading by setting an example? How did people receive your ideas or actions? What do you think would have happened if you had just *told* people to change or improve without taking the first step yourself? Which method would you prefer? Would you like someone *showing* you by their example or *telling* you what to do?

Keywords: Observe, exemplify, entrust

Affirmation: I am an inspiration to others.

18

No rules means no opposition, thereby creating the freedom to be

"All good things are wild, and free."
—HENRY DAVID THOREAU

The Mouse, the Frog, and the Hawk

A mouse and a frog were friends. The mouse could live only on land, whereas the frog could live both on land and in water. The frog said to the mouse, "You are such a good friend; I want you to be with me always." So the frog tied them together by the leg with a piece of thread. On dry land all went well, but upon coming to a pool, the frog jumped in, taking the mouse with him. Alas, the mouse could not swim and died. The dead mouse floated to the top of the pool and was spotted by a hawk. The hawk came down and flew away with the mouse. Sadly, the frog could not untie the thread in time and was also eaten up by the hungry hawk.

WoW: Who you are is good by nature. You are whole and complete. You were born that way. You don't need rules of life, you need to just express yourself. Rules are limiting; being able to express yourself is freeing. If there's a rule in place, it's usually because some people, sometime, forgot who they were—they thought they were *special* and forgot they were like *everyone*. Being special makes you different, which is unfortunate, as we're all the same—that is, we are love, and we are all source, or divine beings. Thinking of yourself as *not* a divine being has you not living from your heart, and some rule is put in place to try to help you return to yourself, like "I must make lots of friends." But along the way, we forgot what the rule was for and lost the whole purpose of it. So to fix *that,* another rule was put in place. Now, with so many rules, most of us are lost in the game and have forgotten even that it *is* a game. Living without rules, as long as you haven't forgotten who you are, allows for freedom.

Activity: Select a game or sport that can be played in teams (example: soccer, tennis, basketball, etc.). With the help of your friends and an adult facilitator, change the rules of the game a little, or change the game completely. Enjoy the renovated or newly invented game.

Explore: Was the experience of the game any different from before? Did it matter to you that you played a game not in accordance with rules already spelled out by someone else? Could you still play any game with a new set of rules? Would you be open to making changes in other areas of your life? Why?

Keywords: Responsible, virtuous, prudent

Affirmation: I always have a choice.

19

Living with no attachment to outside approval is satisfying

"Do not look for approval except for the consciousness of doing your best."

—ANDREW CARNEGIE

The Hare with Many Friends

There lived a hare that was very popular with the other animals, and they all claimed to be his friends. He considered himself "special" for having such support. One day, while he was playing alone, he heard the hounds approaching and hoped to escape them by asking one of his many animal friends to help him. So the hare went to the horse, and asked, "Horse, my friend, could you please carry me on your back and save me from the hounds?" The horse responded, "I'm sorry, I have important jobs to do for my master. I am sure someone else will be able to help." The hare then went to the bull and said, "Bull, my friend, please chase away the hounds with your horns." "I am very sorry, I have an appointment with a lady," said the bull, "but I am sure that our friend the goat will do what you want." But the goat feared that his herd might get annoyed with him for helping the hare, so he directed him to the ram. So the hare went up to the ram and asked him for help. "Another time, my dear friend," said the ram. "Hounds have been known to eat us as well." So the hare finally approached the calf for help. The calf responded, "So many older animals were unable to help you; how can I, a calf, be of any assistance?" By now, the hounds were closing in on the hare. So he relied on his own speed and ran away from there as fast as he could.

WoW: Birds don't brag that they can fly; they just fly. If you just do what you enjoy doing and stop showing off or trying to be "better" than others, you will enjoy what you do so much more. If you describe to others how good you are at something (or how rich, how lucky, etc.), then you take away from your own experience of it. To add to the truth, you subtract from it. Birds don't need any approval from others to keep flying. They don't create workshops on flying and try to get others to attend! You don't need to do something for anyone's approval; do it for the simple satisfaction of doing it. Ecstasy comes to those who simply "be" and trust their inner voice.

Activity: Take some colorful balloons and hang them from the ceiling, using thread or string. Likewise, choose a few colorful balls and attach them to a pole, using rope or thread. Enjoy playing with the attached balloons and balls. Try throwing the balloons and balls at each other and notice what happens due to this restricted motion.

Explore: How did it feel, playing with the tied-up balloons and balls? Was it as much fun as when the balloons and balls are not tied to something? Was there more freedom or less freedom from attachment? Have you ever experienced your freedom being squelched? How would you feel if someone told you to do something without respecting your choice in the matter?

Keywords: Wisdom, conviction

Affirmation: I respect my freedom and privileges.

20

Go with the flow and accept what is in front of you

"The goal of life is to make your heartbeat match the beat of the universe, to match your nature with Nature."

—JOSEPH CAMPBELL

The Lion and the Hare

A lion was very hungry and was looking for food. He saw a hare, fast asleep. As the lion was about to eat her, he saw a stag passing by. The lion thought, "The stag looks bigger and juicier than this hare. Let me eat the stag instead." So he chased the stag. He chased and he chased and he chased, but the stag ran much faster and got away. The lion decided, "Oh, well, I had better go and get the hare now. I am really hungry." When the lion got back to where the hare had been, there was no hare, and he had to go without dinner. He said to himself, "I should've been satisfied with what I had, instead of going after the stag."

WoW: When birds fly, they're not *trying* to fly, they just fly! Striving, or trying, is an illusion. Try to put your shoes on. You'll find that either you do put your shoes on, or you don't. There's no trying. There's also no success or failure. Not putting on your shoes has a successful result: you *didn't* put on your shoes! Putting on your shoes is a successful result: you *did* put on your shoes. There is no trying; there is no failure (and, therefore, no success). Stop checking in on yourself to see what kind of job you did. Don't bother. You're either going to approve or disapprove of what you did, and either notion has judgments. The bird doesn't say to himself, "Wow, look at how well I'm flying!" When he flies without judgment, he disappears. When you simply do what you do when you're doing it, you, too, disappear—life is lived effortlessly. When judgment disappears, all the striving disappears with it. When all the thinking about whether you're doing a good job or not disappears, you live life easily. The stress is gone. When you're on a roller coaster, you don't get out of your seat; you go along for the ride. You are on the ride of life—sit back and enjoy it. Don't get out of your seat!

Activity: Get together with friends and, with the help of an adult, select a recipe that calls for several raw ingredients (such as carrots, beans, tofu, herbs, broth, oil, salt, etc.) that can be cooked in a slow-cooker or crock pot. Follow the recipe, and once all the ingredients are in the pot, put the lid on, add heat, and let the ensemble do what it is supposed to do. Perhaps you may open the lid to check the progress; and even take a taste halfway through the cooking process. Compare the taste of the raw ingredients and the half-cooked ones. Eagerly expect to see how these raw ingredients get transformed into a tasty dish with you just assembling the ingredients and providing the necessary environment for the cooking process.

Explore: Who do you think actually cooked the food? Was it you or something/someone else? Could the absence of one of the elements have made the dish possible? What do you think was that invisible "something" that aided in your efforts? Do you think that striving a little more might have helped in speeding up the cooking process? Why?

Keywords: Arriving, presence, happening

Affirmation: I am grateful for the air I breathe in this moment.

21

To master the mysterious give up trying to figure it out

"Wherever I go, I meet myself."

—Tozan

The Bug and the Bull

A small bug flew and landed on one of the horns of a huge bull. She rested for quite a while on the bull, and just before getting ready to fly away, she asked the bull, "Do you mind if I go now?" The bull raised his eyes lazily and responded, "I didn't notice when you came, and will not know when you leave."

WoW: If you can't hold on to the Tao, the way to be connected to it is to not hold on to it; let it be. Let what be? Nothing. Everything. As soon as you cling to anything, you have left everything (or nothing). You have made something important. Nothing is important. Look at a barrel of ten thousand marbles. If you cling to one particular marble, you've lost the barrel. The wholeness has disappeared. Look at a field of flowers. If you zero in on one flower, the field disappears. When you give up making the Tao something, it becomes what it is: nothing. There's the beauty. There's the radiance.

Activity: Get together with friends and invite an adult to facilitate this activity. Choose your favorite spots to sit down. Draw whatever you feel like, and color the drawing in any way you wish. There are no rules, and there is no requirement to consult anyone. Celebrate the variety of ideas, colors, and talent that went into each individual creation.

Explore: Why did you choose this particular idea for your drawing? What made you choose the colors that you chose? What or who inspired you to complete this drawing? Have you seen that person, thing, or idea? Where do you think these ideas came from?

Keywords: Sacred, invisible, omnipresent

Affirmation: I allow brilliant ideas to flow through me.

22

Palm trees survive hurricanes because they yield to the force

"What you resist persists."

—CARL JUNG

The Ant and the Grasshopper

In a field one summer day, a grasshopper was hopping about, chirping and singing to its heart's content. An ant passed by, carrying an ear of corn on its back to its nest. "Why not come and sing with me," said the grasshopper, "instead of toiling and moiling in that way?" "I am helping to store up food for the winter," said the ant, "and I recommend you do the same." "Why bother about winter?" said the grasshopper. "We have got plenty of food at present." But the ant went on and continued its work. When winter arrived, the grasshopper had no food and was cold and very hungry. He saw the ants distributing corn and other grain they had collected in the summer. The grasshopper mused to himself, "The ants sure know how to use their summer months. Look at them; they are so satisfied and relaxed, enjoying their every moment of winter."

WoW: Being flexible is about being able to quickly and easily adapt to your surroundings. If someone is angry at you for something you did, being flexible might include a simple "I'm sorry", instead of something like defending or explaining yourself—even if you *are* right! The flexible "I'm sorry" immediately eases the anger; there's no pushing back; there's no force. Your flexibility creates that ease. Being flexible is, interestingly, also about being strong. It takes strength to yield willingly, for it shows your ability to put aside your opinions and really observe and experience what's going on. Nature is full of examples of this. For example, trees that can bend in a hurricane survive; those that are stiff fall over. Be flexible, and you'll get through any storm.

Activity: Do this exercise where you are sitting on a chair, maybe at a dining table, and are holding a cup of water in your hands. Now your friend or an adult gradually moves this cup away from you by a few inches every ten seconds or so; and you try to reach for this cup of water with the condition that you will not bend your back. Observe how difficult this becomes until at one point you will not be able to even touch the edge of the cup. Now flex the rules a bit and introduce the condition that you can now bend your back while reaching for the cup of water. Notice how you try to achieve this by flexing and stretching your hand forward. Depending on the size of the table, you may find that you will have to be stretched out flat on the table in order to reach the cup!

Explore: Would you have been able to reach the cup if you had refused to bend and flex your body? Would you have been able to retrieve the cup if you had decided to keep your spine straight? Did you find it favorable to be flexible? In what other areas of your life does it pay to be flexible?

Keywords: Relaxation, resiliency

Affirmation: I choose to be flexible and to go with the flow.

23

The nature of water allows it to take the shape of its container

"If I accept the sunshine and warmth, then I must also accept the thunder and lightning."

—KAHLIL GIBRAN

The Mule

One day a mule began to jump and run about rather impatiently. She was convinced that she could outrun any animal at any speed. "My mother was a racehorse," she thought, "and I can run just as fast!" The mule started running. She ran and ran until she was huffing and puffing. Then she suddenly remembered, "Oh, but my father was a donkey!"

WoW: Things pass; they come and go. Anger passes; upsets pass. If you simply *allow* this, you will be at peace. If you think a rainy day ruins your plans, you have attached yourself to your plans, and you leave little room for satisfaction. To be at peace at all times, be the observer of the universe; appreciate the happenings. None of it means anything—it is *itself*, expressing itself, and *you* are privileged to witness the miracle.

Activity: Have an adult fill a medium- to large-sized box with a variety of different items (balls, dolls, wooden blocks, canvas, ropes, etc.). You and your friends take turns, randomly picking out three items from this box and constructing whatever comes to mind with those three things using aids such as crayons, pencils, glue, and so on (provided separately). You may even depict a story with these creations! Celebrate what your nature intended.

Explore: What led you to create what you created? Who was the silent helper that nudged you on to complete this unplanned project? Did you enjoy the experience of being spontaneous? Did you enjoy creating something you did not plan or were not familiar with before? If so, how?

Keywords: Gentleness, cyclical, spontaneity

Affirmation: I welcome the unknown.

24
Excess of anything does not serve

"Neither a lofty degree of intelligence nor imagination nor both together go to the making of genius. Love, love, love, that is the soul of genius."
—WOLFGANG AMADEUS MOZART

The Fox and the Cat

A fox was boasting to a cat, saying, "I have a whole bag of tricks, which contains a hundred ways of escaping my enemies." "I have only one," said the cat; "but I can generally manage with that." Just at that moment they heard the loud barking of a pack of hounds coming towards them, and the cat immediately scampered up a tree and hid herself in the branches. "This is my plan," said the cat. "What are you going to do?" The fox thought first of one way, then of another, and then of another and another; and while he was debating, the hounds came nearer and nearer. At last, the fox in his confusion was trapped by the hounds. The cat, who had been looking on, said, "Better one safe way than a hundred risky ways!"

WoW: There is a lot of evidence that excess doesn't work in line with the Tao and is not in line with the intended design. A few examples will illustrate the point: if you keep filling a glass, it will overflow; if you're making a campfire, too much wood can actually choke the fire and put it out; swimming too long makes your skin quite wrinkly; laughing too much can make you out of breath and exhausted; eating too much healthy food can make you sick; staying on a roller coaster too long can make you dizzy; and on and on. If your actions are in line with the design, then enjoyment is at its utmost. Just be yourself—stay inside your own intended design.

Activity: Take a balloon and start blowing air into it until it bursts. Observe how the excess air harms the balloon. You may also experiment with water: drink as much water as you need to quench your thirst. Now go ahead and try drinking another glass. See how you feel.

Explore: Do you believe that the excess was useful? In what other areas of your life do you have excesses? What are some ways to eliminate them? How do you think your life will be without excess? Can you be grateful for what you have?

Keywords: Generosity, gratitude

Affirmation: I choose to live in moderation and say no to excess.

25

Viewing yourself as great makes you great

"The greatest danger for most of us is not that our aim is too high and we miss it, but that it is too low and we reach it."

—MICHELANGELO

The Vain Jackdaw

One day in the jungle, a dark, glossy jackdaw found some peacock feathers on the ground. He said to himself, "I'll look more beautiful if I wear these feathers." Saying this, he stuck some of them among his own feathers, left his own flock, and joined the peacocks. As soon as the peacocks saw him, they knew that he was not their kind, so they pecked him with their sharp beaks and drove him away. The jackdaw felt sad and returned to his group. "He left us to join the peacocks; he has no right to be here," remarked the other jackdaws. They drove him out, saying, "If you had been happy with how nature made you, you wouldn't have been attacked by the peacocks or been disrespected by your own kind."

WoW: Imagine yourself—your talents, qualities, and the things you think about. Do you realize that out of the more than seven billion people on Earth, you're the only one who has this combination of qualities? Not only does that make you unique, that makes you great! You are a being with a special place in this world. The biggest obstacle to your recognizing and experiencing your own greatness is your thought that you're not! All you need to do is turn your thoughts to confirm your greatness. There's no evidence for it—it's just who you are. Accept it. Why not?

Activity: Get together with friends and watch this video, *God Would Do a Song and Dance*, by following the website link: http://spiritlibrary.com/spiritual-videos/heavenletters/god-would-do-a-song-and-dance or any other video depicting how you are created in the image of God and that there is no separation between you two. Now form a circle and take turns to name one quality in yourselves that makes you "Great." After this, say out loud together, three times, "I am great no matter what." For the next segment of this activity, name one quality in your friend that makes him or her "Great." Now together, say out loud, three times, "We are great no matter what!"

Explore: How do you view yourself now? Do you think that your worth is equivalent to God's worth? Do you believe that your worth is equivalent to the worth of all of

God's creations, including your friends? Do you feel your connection with all the wondrous creations around you? If so, how?

Keywords: Purity, acknowledgment

Affirmation: You and I are simply grand.

26

See life as an adventure and appreciate all events with calmness

"Remember when life's path is steep to keep your mind even."

—Horace

The Fox and the Mosquitoes

After crossing a river, a fox got its tail entangled in a bush and could not move. A number of mosquitoes, seeing its plight, began biting its tail and thus enjoyed a good meal. A hedgehog strolling by felt sorry for the fox. "You are in a bad situation," said the hedgehog. "Shall I relieve you by driving off those mosquitoes that are sucking your blood?" "Thank you," said the fox, "but I'd rather not." "Why not?" asked the hedgehog. "Well, you see," replied the fox calmly, "these mosquitoes have had their fill; if you drive these away, others will come with fresh appetites and eat me alive."

WoW: Calmness comes from simply observing, not pretending to be caught up in problems outside of you. It *is* pretending, you know! It's playing the game of life. Like in the game of Monopoly, you have a piece to play the game with, like a Top Hat or a Scottie Dog. Life is a game in which the piece is your physical body. In Monopoly, you may have to go to jail. The piece in the *game* has a problem. As the mover of the piece, you are aware it's just a game, and there's no real issue. Outside of Monopoly, you may find yourself in the middle of some problems, but if you remember who you are, you'll remember you're still playing a game, and the "more aware you" has no problems—all is calm. Play the game fully, but don't forget you're really an observer and always at peace.

Activity: Play "What would you do if…?" Create hypothetical circumstances where the expected reaction could look like conflict, difference of opinion, frustration, impatience, or any other undesirable emotion. An adult facilitator poses before each of you such hypothetical questions that might normally evoke negative emotions (for example, "What would you do if your friend hit you?"). You are to take a deep breath and then say, "I have a *choice* and I choose peace; so I will [say what you would do]" (for example, "I will ask my friend what is hurting her so much that she wants to hurt me to make herself feel better").

Explore: How did it feel to choose peace over conflict? Can peace arise from a feeling of unrest or from calmness? Which of these feels better in the body? Why?

Keywords: Peacefulness, knowing, optimism

Affirmation: Peace begins with me.

27

A good person is good to the good and good to the bad

"Turn your gaze inward. Correct yourself and your world will change."

—Kristin Zambucka

The Oxen and the Butchers

Once upon a time, a team of oxen got together. "The butchers slaughter us by the dozen every day," discussed the oxen. "We must do something to stop this." So they decided to take revenge by sharpening their horns and attacking the butchers. While they were busy planning and plotting, an old ox got up on his feet and said, "My brothers, you do have a good reason to dislike the butchers. However, do you understand that this is their job? If you kill these butchers, some other butchers will be sent in tomorrow to continue their job of slaughtering us." The ox continued, "At least these old butchers do their jobs without causing us much pain; how can we be sure that the new guys would do the same?" All the oxen agreed that no matter what they did to the butchers, the world would not go without meat—at least not just yet!

WoW: If you were to travel to a distant planet that had intelligent life on it, and you were the observer (and could remain unseen), everything you saw would be fascinating, new, or at least interesting. There'd be no bad or good. There'd be no right or wrong, for who is judging right and wrong aside from you? It's a journey, an adventure. Okay, let's take this way of observing back to Earth: you have adventures awaiting you at every moment—you may only need a change in your viewpoint to experience what you're doing as an adventure. Be honest, be kind, and be of good spirit. Keep it as the adventure it is. Your life will be exciting and rewarding, and you will find others turned in to the possibility of a similar way of being in their own lives. It can be contagious!

Activity: Get together with your friends and watch the short, inspiring movie on this website: http://www.makeadifferencemovie.com/ or any other movie that teaches that your actions do make a difference. Then choose one person, either in your family or in your friends' circle who you feel has mistreated you or hurt you in some way. Visit this person and say, "I love you no matter what happened in the past." If you have a friendship or peace band/ribbon, pass it on to this person or create one with the words, "Who you are does make a difference."

Explore: How did it feel to be a good friend? Would you like it if someone approached you in the same manner? Is it important to forgive someone who hurt you? Why or why not? What did you like the most about the movie?

Keywords: Trust, empowerment

Affirmation: I have the ability to love unconditionally.

28

Preserve your unique qualities and be an eternally powerful leader

"I want to be all that I am capable of becoming."

—Katherine Mansfield

The Lamp

In a certain household, a beautiful lamp filled with oil burned with a clear, steady light. The more she burned, the more she was swelling with pride at her brightness. "I shine brighter than the sun," said the lamp. Just then a puff of wind came and blew out the light. Someone came and lit the lamp once again, and said, "You just keep shining your light, and never mind the sun; for you are you, and the sun is the sun."

WoW: Perhaps it could be said you are three people: the person you think you are, the person you're afraid you are, and the person who you really are. You aren't who you think you are: if you think you're male (or female) you've limited yourself, because you aren't limited to your gender. If you think you are strong, you've limited your ability to be vulnerable, which is certainly a human trait. If you think you are an understanding person, you might one day find yourself in a situation where you don't understand—how would that seem to you? You would discover you're not always an understanding person! For every way you could describe yourself, it would be useful to recognize that it's a temporary description, not who you are. You're also not the person you're afraid you are: perhaps you're afraid you're weak or shy. You're not that, and you have a fear of being that. The fear doesn't make it true. Who you really are is all things. Not white or black, not a part but the whole, not male or female, not young or old. You are the Tao. Go celebrate who *you* are!

Activity: Get together with friends, but this time play or do any activity, each person by him- or herself, all alone. Let an adult facilitate and support this process. Experience how it feels to be with your own self and not with friends.

Explore: Did you enjoy your own company? Was it easy to come up with ways to engage yourself? Why do you think it is a good idea to be alone every once in a while? How did it feel having your friends around and not interacting with them? What was the one thing that you learned about yourself from this activity?

Keywords: Ingenious, original

Affirmation: I love myself just the way I am.

29

Life unfolds naturally and perfectly, with no need of control

"Know that everything is in perfect order whether you understand it or not."

—VALERY SATTERWHITE

The Fisherman Piping

A fisherman went to the seashore one day to catch some fish. He carried with him some nets and a flute, which he could play very well. At the seashore, he found a nice big, comfortable rock on which to sit and play the flute. His idea was that the music would bring the fish jumping out of the sea, and then he would catch them easily. The fisherman began playing his flute; he played and played and was making wonderful music, but there was still no sign of the fish. Disgusted, the fisherman threw his flute away and cast his net into the sea, and soon found large numbers of fish in his net.

WoW: Imagine you traveled to a distant planet, and you were investigating life there while remaining invisible to the planet's inhabitants. It would be pretty fascinating, and there'd be nothing to "fix," because nothing would be wrong—you'd just be observing what was going on in this new environment. Everything you saw, you would see as "natural." Strange, perhaps, but natural nonetheless. As an observer, you would become both educated and fascinated. The same thing is true of your own life! It's all natural. There's nothing to fix. So now you can do anything, This is known as *inspired* action—action from the "spirit"—which is action born of *being* rather than *doing*. As a pure observer, there's no opinion; there's allowance, acceptance, perfection. You can't improve on what is already perfect.

Activity: Do a guided meditation exercise where you focus on your breath (a suggestion: http://www.danielharper.org/story23.htm), facilitated by an adult. Enjoy the practice of allowing your breath to flow in and out in a natural rhythm.

Explore: How did it feel to not force the breath? Would you like it if you had to breathe at a pace dictated by someone else? Which seems more natural—following your pace or another's? Is it easier to let go rather than to control something? Why or why not? Is it beneficial to be natural?

Keywords: Organic, indigenous

Affirmation: I see the perfection in all.

30

Using power for wrongful deeds weakens you

"When the power of love overcomes the love of power, the world will know peace."

—JIMI HENDRIX

The North Wind and the Sun

One day the north wind and the sun had a debate as to who was stronger. So they decided to try their powers on a traveler, to see who could get him to remove his coat the soonest. The wind went first. He gathered all his might and force and came whirling and swirling furiously at the traveler. The stronger the wind blew, the harder the man held onto his coat for protection from cold. Next it was the sun's turn. He beamed gently on the traveler. The man felt a little warm and took off his coat and put it away, then continued on his journey.

WoW: Force between people is always unnecessary. Imagine your parents want to take you to see some relatives, and you want to stay home to play with your friends. If you put up a fuss and refuse to go, they might use force, like pulling you or carrying you to the car. You cry; your parents are angry. Do you think anyone's going to have a good time at your relatives' house? Even when the force is gone, the hurt, resentment, and anger persist. The little trip is a disaster. This kind of thing can happen with your own friends if they want to play one game and you want to play another—if you use force to get what you want, your friend will probably just go home, and you'll be in a bad mood. The way to experience the happiness is to surrender to what's in front of you—if you're in a boat in a river, it's so much easier to go downstream, going with the flow instead of against it. Even if you don't want to go to your relatives' house or play your friend's game, overall you'll have a much more enjoyable time if you let go of what you want instead of bringing force into the picture. It's never worth it. Force creates counterforce. Wars exist because the adults want things their way. Surrender is ultimate control.

Activity: Get together with friends and have an adult put on a video clip for you that shows some action involving a chase and anger. After this clip, watch an inspirational movie or a video clip that portrays love. Celebrate the differences between the videos you saw.

Explore: Which video did you enjoy the most and why? Would you prefer that someone ask you to do something using love or using force? Which feels better?

Does the world need more love or more force? Are peace and tranquility a direct consequence of love or of force and anger? How so?

Keywords: Tolerance, grace

Affirmation: I am inherently powerful and see no use for force in my life.

31

True nature of man is peace

"We must not bring one war to an end—or thirty—but the idea of war itself."

—Deepak Chopra

The Boys and the Frogs

Some boys were playing on the edge of a pond. They spotted some frogs swimming about in the shallow water and decided to amuse themselves a bit. So the boys picked up some stones and started pelting the frogs with them, just to see who hit the mark and who didn't. At last, one of the frogs spoke up, "Oh, stop! Stop! I beg of you—what is fun for you is death to us."

WoW: If you use a weapon, then by definition you're not being yourself, because you are using something outside yourself. That's being a coward. To remain in touch with your source, you cannot use or be anything but yourself. To harm another with a weapon is a sign that you've lost yourself and are trying to protect your own ego. You've been hurt somehow and don't have the courage to face the hurt, so you protect yourself from the hurt by using outside force—but that's only hiding the hurt. The hurt will remain, and you will go farther from the source. Drop all weapons and become truly brave.

Activity: You and your friends bring in "toy weapons," such as water guns, pistols, swords, arrows, knives, and so on. With the assistance of an adult, demonstrate how these can be put to alternate use. For instance, the water gun could be used to water plants or to clean the indoor artificial plants; an arrowhead could be used as a screw driver; the knife could be used for cutting open boxes, and so on.

Explore: What do you think makes an object a weapon? Did you enjoy finding alternate uses for these aggressive play toys? Do you think that the world can be a better place without weapons? If you cannot find an alternate use for these toys, would you be willing to discard them? Why?

Keywords: Liveliness, civility, friendship

Affirmation: I am at peace with all of God's creations.

32

Connect with the invisible power for perfect harmony

"Do all the good you can. By all the means you can. In all the ways you can. In all the places you can. At all the times you can. To all the people you can. As long as ever you can."

—J OHN W ESLEY

The Farmer and his Sons

A farmer was on his deathbed. Before he died, he wanted to share a secret with his lazy sons. So he called them to his bedside. "My sons, I am about to die. I wish to tell you that there is a treasure hidden in my vineyard. Dig, and you will surely find it," said the farmer. As soon as their father died, the sons took spade and fork and started to dig up the soil of the vineyard. They dug and dug, turning up the soil over and over again. "There is nothing in here," cried the sons. However, after such thorough digging, the vines produced a great crop like never before. This was the hidden treasure!

WoW: Imagine you've decided you're going to always walk only north. Now imagine there's another person who has decided he's always going to walk only south. Now imagine the two of you are on this journey and actually meet, and come to a stop face to face, just like in the story from Dr. Seuss. If you don't step to the side, and the other person also doesn't step to the side, you're stuck there forever! Neither of you gets his way; you're both being stubborn and "right." But if you (or the other) simply yield your position, you both get what you want. This is giving up your rigidity and going with the path of the Tao, the path of what works. There's a "hidden treasure" in living the goodness of the Tao—satisfaction and happiness.

Activity: Play the "predicting" game. Get together with friends and have an adult facilitator give you questions, and you take turns saying what will happen next (example: The question could be, "What happens when you turn off the light at night?" The answer could be, "The room becomes dark" or "I fall asleep"). Observe *how* you are able to tell what might happen next. Some questions could also be abstract!

Explore: Who do you think told you what would happen next? Have you seen that person, thing, or intelligence at work? How many times in the past have you been able to predict correctly, and what were the situations? Do you think everybody has an "invisible friend" that tells them what is about to happen?

Keywords: Openhearted, passionate, joyous

Affirmation: All my problems have already been solved for me.

33

Understanding oneself is wisdom

"I count him braver who overcomes his desires than him who conquers his enemies; for the hardest victory is over self."

—ARISTOTLE

The Man and the Lion

A man and a lion were each other's companions on a journey. In their conversations, each began to boast about their power and strength. The lion said, "I am stronger and more courageous than you men." "No, we are stronger, more courageous, and smarter than you lions," responded the man. As they were walking and arguing, they came to a crossroads where they saw a statue of a man strangling a lion. "There!" said the man triumphantly. "Look at that! Doesn't that prove to you that we are stronger than you?" "Not so fast, my friend," said the lion. "That is only your view. If we lions could make statues, you would surely see the man underneath the lion."

WoW: You know water. It's wet. If someone told you water was mean and angry, you would know that's not true, because you know water. You might even think they were being silly! When you know yourself, you similarly have real wisdom. Others' words or actions don't need to affect you, because you know yourself. When you know yourself, you also know all feelings and reactions are your own creations, and you will never blame others for your thoughts or feelings. You can keep growing, self-exploring, and staying in the flow with the Tao, and you can share who you really are with others.

Activity: Get together with friends and, with the assistance of an adult, write or draw responses on a sheet of paper to questions such as, "How are you feeling right now?" "Are you mad at someone?" and so on, which are aimed at directing your attention inward. After you finish the worksheet, you share your answers with the group. Before you begin sharing, you must declare out loud, "I am fully responsible for this and blame nobody."

Explore: Did this exercise help you understand yourself better? How did it feel to take 100 percent of the responsibility for the way you feel about yourself and others? How would you feel if people stopped blaming you for their problems? Did you find this activity easy or challenging? Why so?

Keywords: Strength, immortality

Affirmation: I create my own reality.

34
Greatness is not achieved by domination

"Do you wish people to think well of you? Don't speak well of yourself."

—BLAISE PASCAL

The Two Pots

Once two pots—one made of clay and the other of brass—were carried together on a river tide. The clay pot was the more delicate of the two. "Please stay close to me," said the brass pot. "You will be safe, as I am stronger and will protect you." "Thank you," responded the clay pot, "but if I do, then I am bound to crack. I'd rather float to safety alone than come near you and risk being broken."

WoW: Did you ever hear someone say "Trust me"? Did that make you think that maybe you shouldn't? Gravity is a master teacher—it never says, "Trust me"; it never even tells you its rules—it allows you to discover them for yourself. It applies any consequence without exception. Yet it earns your great respect. If you fall, gravity doesn't gloat. You're allowed to get up and try again. If one of your rules is "I'll let it be," then you will easily earn great respect too, for there's no ego in that rule, only grace.

Activity: Watch the video clip of a lion named Christian on the website link http://www.metacafe.com/watch/1465395/christian_the_lion_the_full_ _in_hq/, where he reunites with his caretakers. Alternately, you may search for "Christian the lion" on http://www.youtube.com. Appreciate the greatness of the moment, even though no words were exchanged.

Explore: What was the greatness factor in this video clip? What touched you the most about this video? Is it necessary to speak many words or show material accomplishments in order to be great? Why or why not?

Keywords: Sanctity, stewardship

Affirmation: I lead by example.

35
Happiness is felt only when its presence within us is acknowledged

"Gratitude is not only the greatest of virtues, but the parent of all the others."

—MARCUS TULLIUS CICERO

The Rooster and the Pearl

A rooster was once prancing about on a farm among the hens, when suddenly he spotted something shiny and bright amid the straw. "Ho! Ho!" he cried, "that's for me!" He scratched around and soon got it out from underneath the straw. It turned out to be a pearl that by some chance had been lost in the yard. "You may be a treasure," sang the rooster, "to people that treasure you, but as for me, I would be more grateful for a single grain of barley than a peck of pearls."

WoW: The "purpose" of a car is transportation—to take you from one place to another. Imagine the car thinks its purpose is to get to the next gas or petrol station to fill up. Now its true purpose is lost, and the journey becomes one of a chore. Some people are like that. Their true purpose may be to serve, to love unconditionally. But if they *think* their true purpose is something else, their real purpose becomes lost. For example, suppose you're excited about going to visit some people you love. On the way, you pass a store and stop there for a snack. If stopping for the snack becomes your new purpose, then the original purpose has been lost. You had a snack. It was satisfying. But now what? If you have forgotten your original purpose, you might even turn around and go home and wonder why you aren't fully satisfied. Your *true* purpose got lost. Had you remembered that the stopping at the store was part of the journey to spend a day visiting, you would be grateful for the snack *and* be excited about continuing the trip. The journey is all of it. Have a good trip, and give thanks for it!

Activity: Get together with your friends for a meal or snack, and practice mindful eating. Savor not only the taste of your favorite foods, but also notice the textures. Give a silent appreciation for the person who cooked that article of food and to the one who grew the ingredients that went into your dish. Revel in the long (seemingly unending) chain of people and resources that went into bringing that food to you.

Explore: Did the food taste any different as a result of this exercise? Now that you can see the long chain of people and resources that bring you your food, do you feel grateful for all your meals? Why do you think it is important for us to pay attention to everything that we use or consume? What other things in your life could you pay closer attention to?

Keywords: Contentment, bliss

Affirmation: I am filled with joy, and I spread cheer all around me.

36

To naturally flourish, do not try to get attention

"If I could I would always work in silence and obscurity, and let my efforts be known by their results."

—Emily Brontë

The Fighting Rooster and Eagle

Two roosters were fighting about who was the better between them. They fought and fought, and after a while one of them defeated the other. The one that was badly beaten hid himself in a nearby hole. The victorious rooster ran up and perched himself in a high place, from where he was visible to all. An eagle spotted him and swooped down, picked him up in his claws, and carried him away. The rooster that was hiding saw what had just happened and came out of the hole. He forgot all about his recent loss and walked about, fearlessly.

WoW: You can't have "left" without also having "right." "Left" exists only with "right." This duality exists everywhere. So if you say you're upset, you must also have its opposite present (perhaps peacefulness) in your experience, for how would you know you're upset unless you have something to compare it against? People who have to prove themselves by showing off are usually the loneliest of people, since the need to show off comes from a feeling of not being known or appreciated for who they are. People who feel known are satisfied and do not need to show off what they already have within themselves. People who are showing off are putting effort into trying to feel connected, but that usually doesn't work, because the effort makes it appear unnatural. To feel connected, don't show off; rather, appreciate your surroundings and simply know you're part of the whole. The feeling of connectedness will surface by your being interested, not interesting.

Activity: Get together with your friends and, with the assistance of an adult, cook a pot of chili or soup or make some savory pancakes. Prepare half the soup without adding any salt, or make the pancakes with very little sugar. Appreciate the importance of salt (and sugar) in these dishes, for without the salt or sugar, you can hardly taste the heartiness of the other ingredients. Revel in the fact that although you can see most of the ingredients, the one that makes the dish fulfilling is the obscure and invisible saltiness or sweetness.

Explore: In what ways can you appreciate or recognize someone who is in the background and not as accomplished as some others? Would you see your greatness even if you do not have any material or academic recognitions? Would you want to be like the salt in the soup and help bring out others' greatness? Can you think of other obscure ingredients in the foods you normally eat?

Keywords: Dichotomy, endurance

Affirmation: I am a blessing to those whose lives I touch.

37

The world can transform itself using minimal efforts to change

"If you want to build a ship, don't drum up people together to collect wood and don't assign them tasks and work, but rather teach them to long for the endless immensity of the sea."

—Antoine de Saint-Exupery

The Fox Without a Tail

A fox once fell into a trap. After a lot of struggling, he managed to get free; but at a high cost—he had lost his tail in the struggle with the trap! He felt very ashamed of his appearance and very badly wanted the other foxes to also part with their tails. He thought, "If the other foxes gave up their tails, then I would fit right in with the rest." So he called a meeting of all the foxes, and advised them to cut off their tails: "They're ugly things," he said, "and also heavy and tiresome to always carry around." Hearing this, one of the foxes replied, "My friend, your life will be less complicated without that lousy tail. You are fortunate indeed."

WoW: Life itself has no right or wrong; that's made by people's opinions, and it may seem to you like your opinions are the right ones. But everyone else has opinions as well, and they think their opinions are the right ones (and therefore yours are wrong). You can see that with billions of people in the world, this can lead to a real mess. If you just know that you, and everyone, simply have opinions, you'll soon discover there's no right or wrong to them; they simply exist. So it's not useful to try to change others to take on your opinions any more than it's useful for them to try to make you take on theirs! True peace and calmness come if you simply allow your opinions and those of others to be voiced—neither has to be evaluated!

Activity: Go to the beach or a sandbox and hold some sand in your hands. See what happens when you simply have your hands cupped versus when you squeeze your hands. Notice that when you squeeze (i.e., do something), the sand slips out through your fingers; the same can be experimented with water as well. Celebrate the fact that when you do not *do* much, something gets done (in this case, the sand or water stays within your cupped hands).

Explore: In what other situations in your life can you accomplish more by trying less? Imagine you had a puppy or kitten in your hands; what do you think would happen if you squeezed it tightly? How would you prefer for others to deal with you: by forcing you to do something, or by allowing you to be? Why so?

Keywords: Quietness, retreating, eagerness

Affirmation: I get more done by trying less.

38

A person living his true nature is never aware of it

"Never apologize for showing feeling. When you do so, you apologize for the truth."

—BENJAMIN DISRAELI

The Crab and His Mother

An old crab said to her son, "Why do you walk sideways like that, my son? You must learn to walk straight." The young crab replied, "Show me how, mom, and I'll follow your example." The old crab tried walking straight; she tried a few times but was unable to. Then she suddenly realized how foolish she was to be finding fault with her child's manner of walking. "We crabs never walk straight," recollected the mother crab.

WoW: Have you ever noticed that the only people who are trying to be happy are people who are not happy? People who are already happy needn't *try* to be happy! They simply *are* happy! You don't need to try to be what you already are; it happens naturally. If you try to be good, you are, by definition, not being good (in that moment). Trying to be something means you're not already being that. Otherwise, why try? If you were already in a good mood, would you try to be in a good mood? Or if you were feeling silly, would you try to be silly? Of course not. A truly good person need not do anything to be good. It's simply in his nature.

Activity: Visit any zoo or farm where there are a few different species of animals. Observe how they are simply being true to their nature, without trying to pretend to be someone or something else.

Explore: Would you prefer going to a zoo with real animals or to a zoo where humans are dressed as animals? Which would seem more natural? Which might produce a sense of wonderment and lasting joy in you? Why so? Why do you think many of us like to be around people and things that are true to their own nature?

Keywords: Genuineness, goodness

Affirmation: I acknowledge and appreciate the unique talents of each person.

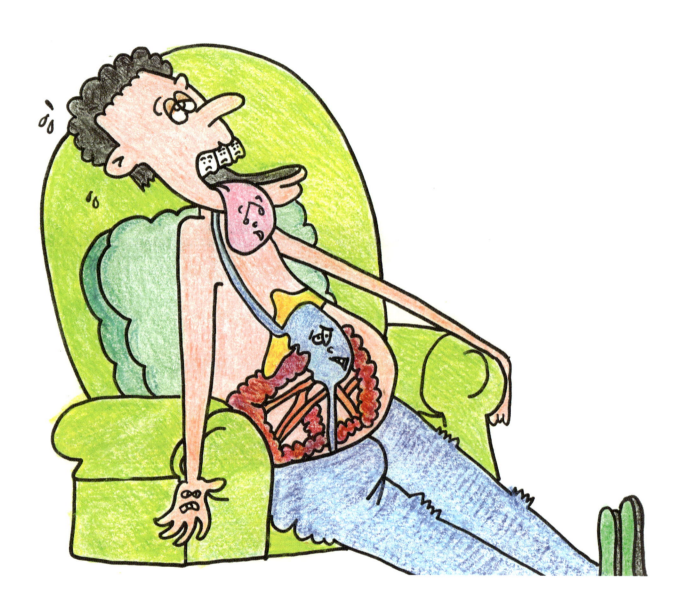

39

You are a part of the whole

"What is in one is in the whole, and therefore, ultimately, each soul is responsible for the whole world."

—GARY ZUKAV

The Belly and the Members

One fine day, when all the members of the body were busy doing their jobs, it suddenly occurred to them that while they were doing all the work, the belly was getting all the food. So they held a meeting, and after a long discussion, they decided, "We will stop all work until the belly agrees to take its proper share of the work." So for a day or two, the hands refused to pick up food, the mouth refused to receive it, and the teeth refused to chew. But then the members began to find that they themselves were not feeing active: the hands could hardly move, the mouth was all parched and dry, and the legs were unable to support the rest of the body. They finally realized that even the belly, in its own quiet way, was doing necessary work for the body—and that all must work together, or the body would go to pieces.

WoW: If you see yourself as part of everything, you'll never be lacking anything. On the other hand, if you see yourself as separate or as special, you'll always be lacking. If you see yourself as belonging to everything, then you'll always feel fulfilled. If you see yourself as separate, you will always feel empty or needy. Everything is complete as is; nothing is lacking. If you think something is lacking, you'll try to add to it—but just as adding a log to a well-burning fire may actually choke it, or adding to the truth subtracts from it, adding to what's complete makes it incomplete. Don't interfere with the Tao.

Activity: Play with play-doh of many different colors. Identify the individual colors, and then take a tiny piece of each color and mix it up to make a homogeneous mass of one color. Celebrate the many individual pieces that made up the whole. You may also experiment with various colors of paint. For instance, you can make the color green by mixing yellow and blue. Notice how the individual colors merge or dissolve into the whole (one color).

Explore: Could the one "whole" have been created without the individual pieces of play-doh or paint? In what other areas have you found that small pieces indeed make up a larger whole? Do you believe you are an individual piece of the whole of humanity? Do you consider yourself an important entity of the whole? If so, how?

Keywords: Equality, interconnection

Affirmation: I am an important member of the universe, and my loving thoughts benefit all.

40

Surrender to the invisible creator

"You win the victory when you yield to friends."

—SOPHOCLES

Hercules and Pallas

Hercules was once traveling along a narrow roadway when he came across a strange-looking animal that raised its head and threatened him. Hercules fearlessly gave him a few blows with his club and moved on. The monster, however, much to the astonishment of Hercules, grew three times bigger and appeared a lot more threatening. Hercules now gave the monster twice as many blows as before, but the harder and quicker he struck him, the bigger and more frightful grew the monster. Now it completely filled up the road. Just then the Goddess Pallas appeared upon the scene. "Stop, Hercules!" she said. "Stop your blows! The monster's name is Strife. Leave it alone, and it will soon become as little as it was at first."

WoW: The instant we are born, we're on a journey to return to where we came from. What you do with this journey is up to you, so enjoy it. Imagine two babies born on the same day, placed in the same hospital room in their beds, facing each other. They go on and live their lives, and let's say eighty years later they're in a hospital on their deathbeds. They happen to be in the same room, facing each other. One says to the other, "So? How was it for you?" Although this is light and somewhat humorous, the point is that they're now ready to return to the source, and one is simply inquiring how the journey was. The journey is all we have this time around. So go enjoy! Let things happen; surrender to the ride home.

Activity: Play "Tag, you're it!" with your friends. While being chased, deliberately slow down every now and then for your friend to be able to tag you easily. Celebrate your friendship based on yielding and allowing, rather than resisting and chasing.

Explore: How did it feel to be the one who was able to tag your friend effortlessly? How did it feel to be the one who slowed down for the friend to catch up easily? How do you think such actions can affect friendships? Do you think our world could use more people who surrender rather than guard themselves? Why?

Keywords: Gracious, transient

Affirmation: I choose cooperation over competition.

41

Appearances may be deceptive

"The moment one gives close attention to any thing, even a blade of grass, it becomes a mysterious, awesome, indescribably magnificent world in itself."

—Henry Miller

The Horse and the Donkey

A horse and a donkey were traveling together. The horse was happily trotting about in its beautiful ornamental covering, whereas the donkey was carrying, with great difficulty, heavy articles in a large basket slung across its back. "I wish I were you," sighed the donkey, "with nothing to do, well fed, and wearing all that finery!" The next day, however, there was a great battle, and the horse was badly wounded. His friend the donkey remarked, "I'm so glad to be safe in my own skin!"

WoW: There is no "in" without "out" or left without right; there is also no wisdom without ignorance. The wiser something is, the more likely you will find someone making fun of it. People laughed at the "discovery" that the world was round, for they "knew" it was flat. People thought Jesus was evil and threatening. Turn this around and notice the things *you* make fun of—perhaps there's great wisdom in those things. Perhaps.

Activity: Get together with friends and plan ahead to be dressed in clothes of the same color. Each of you tells the adult facilitator what you are the most skilled in performing (example: singing, dancing, mimicry, painting, juggling, yoga asana, etc.). The adult writes them down on small pieces of paper, folds them, and places them inside a bowl. You take turns picking out a piece of this folded paper and perform whatever is written on it. Celebrate the fact that although you are all dressed in the same color, you are each talented differently; and even if you feel goofy, you are truly magnificent.

Explore: Do you believe it is important to look beyond someone's appearance? Why or why not? Is it certain that two people with the same external characteristics have the same talents too? In what ways are you and your friend similar, and in what ways are you different? Are you willing to accept yourself and others, despite the "silliness" or "imperfections"?

Keywords: Loving, feeling, insightful

Affirmation: I am perfect just the way I am.

42

Come together as one and gain

"How is it they live in such harmony the billions of stars—when most men can barely go a minute without declaring war in their minds about someone they know."

—SAINT THOMAS AQUINAS

The Lion and the Mouse

Once when a lion was fast asleep, a tiny mouse was walking up and down his belly. This woke the lion up, and he placed his huge paw on this tiny mouse and opened his jaws to swallow him. "Sorry, my dear King," cried the little mouse. "Forgive me this time. Who knows—I may be able to return this favor someday." The lion was so tickled at the idea of the mouse being able to help him that he lifted up his paw and let him go. Some days later, the lion was caught in a trap laid out by some hunters. They had just gone in search of a wagon to carry the lion, when the tiny mouse saw the lion in trouble and came up to rescue him. The mouse gnawed the ropes that bound the lion, setting him free. "Wasn't I right, your majesty?" said the tiny mouse.

WoW: The Tao is like the Big Bang (the beginning of the universe)—it gives birth to everything. It starts with one thing, which continues to grow and gives birth to more things. Everything, including you, comes into existence from the source. Everything eventually returns to the source. This is the journey. Where is there room for violence? What is its purpose? Violence comes from thinking you're special and not knowing how to get your personal needs met, so in frustration you have your own little explosion. When you're in harmony with everything, then you have no personal needs, so there is no need for (or expression of) any violence. If you let go of any material things, you're freer, so you gain by losing the "importance" of things. But if you hold onto material things, your life focus is more toward protecting and keeping those things than it is toward simply living life, so you lose out. When you do not feel you need anything, then you're in harmony with everything.

Activity: Do a role-playing exercise where you pair up with a friend and follow a script that your adult facilitator has prepared for you. The script will reflect a dialogue between two people, where one is trying to be *right* and the other one is trying to be *kind*. You and your partner take turns playing both roles. You will experience (through this role-playing dialogue) how it feels to be with someone who wants to be right versus one who wants to be kind—and also how it feels when *you* are being right versus being kind.

Explore: Which feels better, being right or being kind? Which feels better, being with someone who wants to be right or with someone who is kind? What do you think you will gain if you release the need to be right? What do you choose to be in your life, right or kind? Why?

Keywords: Agreement, forgiveness

Affirmation: I am kind to others and am surrounded by people who are kind to me.

43

The truly powerful go about easily and effortlessly

"A good heart is better than all the heads in the world."

—EDWARD BULWER-LYTTON

The Fir Tree and the Thorny Bush

A fir tree was boasting to a thorny bush, "You poor creature, you are of no use to anyone. Look at me. I am useful when men want to build houses; they can't do without me." The thorny bush replied, "Ah, that's great: but when they come with axes and saws to cut you down, you'd wish you were a thorny bush and not a fir."

WoW: There's an interesting and fun exercise that shows the grace of life. Imagine fifty people standing in an empty room, all following the simple instruction, "Move into the spot that has the most space." You would see what looks like a continuous random movement, since the spot with the most space keeps moving its location as well. But this movement of people has a purpose, a flow, an ease. Nobody bumps into anyone else, and they're all in harmony and partnership. They're all moving like water moves. Water never bumps into a large rock, it flows easily around it. When you live your life like you're moving toward the place with the most room, people will notice your ease with life and will want to naturally be able to do that too. You will be teaching softness without doing anything but living softly. That's very satisfying and moving.

Activity: Play the game "Simon says." In this game, your adult facilitator gives you various instructions, such as jump, hop on one leg, and so on. *Only* if the instructions are preceded by the phrase, "Simon says…" must you act out the instruction. Along with some easier commands, he or she may ask you to do something that may not be very natural for you, such as to stand on your toes, walk on your heels, or stand upside down. Observe how some things are easier to do than others.

Explore: Which tasks were easy, and which were not? Did you have to think or pay more attention before following the commands that were easy or those that were difficult? Which is wiser to do—the easy or the difficult tasks? Why so?

Keywords: Power, quietude

Affirmation: My gentleness is my strength.

44

Give up the need for more, and know when to stop

"Trust yourself. You know more than you think you do."
—BENJAMIN SPOCK

The Fox and the Grapes

One hot summer day, a fox was strolling through an orchard. There he saw a bunch of delicious-looking grapes, hanging from a vine. "Just the right thing to quench my thirst," remarked the fox. Going back a few paces, he took a running start and jumped, but he missed the grapes. Turning around again, with a one, a two, and a three, the fox once again reached for the grapes, but they were too high up for the fox to reach. Again and again he tried, but could not succeed. Finally he made peace with the situation, saying, "Maybe those grapes are sour, and that's why I couldn't reach them."

WoW: Did you ever play a video game that was challenging? You play and play and eventually win the game. This brings a feeling of satisfaction. But often what happens is that you now think that the source of satisfaction is in the winning of the video game, rather than recognizing that your own perseverance, determination, and commitment are the source. These qualities are available anywhere in life, but because you misidentified the source as the video game, you play more and more video games, looking for that satisfaction. Unfortunately, you seldom get it! But it's not in the game, it's in *you*! So you can get lost in your games and lose contact with family, friends, work, play, and adventure. Eventually, you discover for yourself that real satisfaction lies elsewhere, where you're sharing yourself and being with others. There's a saying: "You can never get enough of what you don't really want." The source of satisfaction is never in things. Learn to stop; give up the attachments. Participate. Be satisfied.

Activity: Set a goal of how much you'd like to save in your piggy bank. You may choose to save a specified number of coins or a certain amount of money. Once you achieve your goal, stop and give half of the money away to someone or some cause that requires it more than you do. Enjoy practicing when to stop.

Explore: How did you feel when you first started the project and when it was time to finish it? Was it easy to know when to stop collecting money and actually stop?

Would it have been easier to stop if you had not declared at the beginning when you would stop? In what other areas can you apply this principle and benefit?

Keywords: Prioritize, abundance

Affirmation: I let go of wanting more and am thankful for what I have.

45
Not outward grandeur, but peace of mind is true accomplishment

"You can outdistance that which is running after you, but not what is running inside you."

—Rwandan Proverb

The Donkey in the Lion's Skin

One day a donkey found a lion's skin and put it on. She pretended to be a lion, the king of the jungle, and frightened all the animals she came across. When a fox came along, and she tried to frighten him, he said, "If I hear a lion roar, then I'll really be scared; but if he brays, whatever he may wear, I will not be scared."

WoW: There is no such thing as stupid or imperfect except when comparing it to something from your past or to something you already know. Look at this shape, which we'll call a zwurfe: ଔ—is it perfect or imperfect? A good zwurfe or a bad one? You probably say either that you don't know, as there's nothing to compare it with, or that it is perfect, because you see nothing wrong with it! But what if you're shown a second zwurfe, like this: ನ? Which one (if either) is perfect? How about *this* shape called a circle: ✸—is it perfect or imperfect? The circle is imperfect because of your knowledge of how a circle "should" look. But *inherently*, without past, without knowing, they're both neither imperfect nor bad. They just *are*. They are pure. Now see everything in your life like this. The only imperfection you may see is a quality *you* give it, not one *it* has. The imperfection comes into existence in your comparisons. Knowing this enables you to see beyond the surface. You gain the ability to see perfection in anything, because it is inherently whole.

Activity: Do a fun activity called "Looking for perfection." Go out in nature and notice what most people would normally term imperfect or defective, and invite an adult to ask you, "Why is *that* perfect?" An example would be to see a fruit that has not ripened in time, and your responses might be, "So that nobody plucks it," or "It will be ready when we are ready in the future," or "The color on it makes it look beautiful," and so on. Enjoy discovering perfection in the seemingly imperfect.

Explore: Is it sensible to notice perfection in everything? Why or why not? How would such an attitude change your world and your experience in it? Do you experience a sense of peacefulness when you love and accept yourself and everything in nature as it is?

Keywords: Perfection, nonjudgmental, tranquil

Affirmation: I live in a perfect world.

46
Heaven on Earth is guaranteed for the content at heart

"While we pursue happiness, we flee from contentment."

—Hasidic Proverb

The Lion and the Boar

One very hot summer day, a lion and a boar came to a little stream at the same moment. They began quarreling as to who should drink first. The quarrel became a fight, and then they started attacking one another. Suddenly, both the lion and the boar noticed some vultures perched on a branch of a tree above them. Both knew at once that the vultures were waiting to fly down and feed upon the remains of whoever was killed in this fight. They at once calmed down and said to each other, "We'd rather make the most of what we have than be eaten by vultures." So the lion and the boar took turns and drank from the stream to their hearts' content.

WoW: You know the secret of happiness? Accepting what is. Peace also comes from accepting what is. Imagine someone making a fervent prayer for happiness. She says, "Please, God, please, oh please, make everything exactly the way that it is!" This person's prayers are instantly granted, and she's happy and at peace. Most people pray for what isn't. When you look at that, you can easily see that they're going to be disappointed, because things are not as they are not! Being content with what *is* is actually pretty easy, because "what is" always totally surrounds you! You're surrounded by peace. You're embraced by the Tao.

Activity: If you have more than one of the same (or similar) toy or book, give it to a friend who does not have one of those. Enjoy playing this swapping game with your group of friends under the facilitation of an adult. If there are any toys or books left over from this exercise, give them to somebody else outside of the group (perhaps a friend or relative). Enjoy the experience of feeling content with having just enough of something.

Explore: How did it feel to share an extra toy or book with your friend? How did it feel receiving a toy or book that you didn't have before? What can you do with some of the other excesses in your life? Do you feel peaceful and content with what you have?

Keywords: Serenity, contribution

Affirmation: I thank the universe for giving me enough to share with others.

47

More can be accomplished by doing less and with less effort

"To accomplish great things, we must not only act, but also dream; not only plan, but also believe."

—Anatole France

The Milkmaid and Her Pail

In a village one morning, Patty the milkmaid was off to market, carrying her milk in a pail on her head. As she went along, she began calculating what she would do with the money she would get for the milk. "I'll buy some hens from farmer Brown," she said, "and they will lay eggs each morning, which I will sell to the pastor's wife. With the money that I get from the sale of these eggs, I'll buy myself a new gown and a hat; and when I go to market, won't all the young men come up and speak to me! Polly Shaw will be so jealous; but I don't care. I shall just look at her and toss my head like this." As she spoke, she tossed her head back, the pail fell off, and all the milk was spilled. So she had to go home and tell her mother what had occurred. "Ah, my child," said the mother, "Don't try this hard; just believe, and your wishes will come true."

WoW: You know how to wake up each morning, right? But do you really? If you didn't set an alarm clock, would you still wake up? If you didn't have someone wake you, you still would wake up; if you were in an enclosed room with no windows, in total darkness, you would wake up. So do you know how you wake up, or do you just wake up? It's your body knowing how to do that. Your body is on the same cycle as the rotation of the Earth, with a twenty-four-hour rhythm. So you are connected to the world's rhythm, which is connected to the universe's rhythm. There's nothing you need to do to wake up, beat your heart, breathe, see, live; you just do so. So there's no need to try to do anything to be better than anything. You are already in the flow of the Tao. Simply enjoy. All is well.

Activity: Do this interesting exercise (adapted from a technique demonstrated by Paul Hoffman at http://www.daysculpting.com) with your friends and under the guidance of an adult. Stand up and extend your right arm in front of you, with the index finger pointing out as well. Now slowly turn as far to the right as you possibly can (keeping your arm extended with finger pointing out and feet pointing forward). You will reach a point where you can go no further; remember that point! Now, return to standing with your arms by your sides. Close your eyes and let your adult facilitator guide you through a visualization exercise, where you imagine that you are as flexible as a rubber band. Try the same exercise one more time and observe how far you are able to go this time.

Explore: Were you able to turn farther the second time around? Why do you think so? Did the results surprise you? How did you feel while you did the visualization? Is it possible to talk to your mind and program it to do more than what you think it can? In what other areas of your life could you use this technique for your benefit?

Keywords: Mystery, connectedness

Affirmation: All my pleasant dreams come true.

48

Accumulating less and letting go are true strengths

"Would people know that nothing can happen unless the entire universe makes it happen, they would achieve much more with less expenditure of energy."

—NISARGADATTA MAHARAJ

The Swollen Fox

Some shepherds had hidden bread and meat in a hollow tree so that they might eat it after their work was done. A hungry fox, passing by the tree, found this delicious food and decided to eat it. So he slipped in through the narrow opening in the tree and greedily ate all the food. When the fox tried getting out, he found that he had swollen up after eating this big meal and could not squeeze out through the hole. After repeated tries, he started whining and groaning, wondering how he landed up in such a mess. Another fox that came that way saw what had happened and said, "Well, my friend, I think that you should wait inside the tree until you return to your normal size; you'll then be able to get out easily." The swollen fox thought to himself, "Alas, I should have known better than to be so greedy; now I must wait for nature to reduce my size!"

WoW: There are many people in the world who are rich. They've spent their lives accumulating money and items like houses, boats, and fancy cars. Many of these people are not truly satisfied and happy in their lives, because their lives have become *about* their wealth, not about their love for people, family, nature, and spirit. They've misidentified the source of satisfaction, and they just can't get enough of what they don't really want. To achieve satisfaction and happiness, do not focus your energy on the accumulation of material things; rather, focus your energy on contribution, your connection to your family and friends, the world, and the Tao.

Activity: Give away two articles of your clothing: one that no longer fits you, and one that you love and are now using regularly. Enjoy and experience the various sensations as you undertake this project of letting go.

Explore: How do you feel about yourself after this project? Do you sense a feeling of lack or of abundance? Is it easier to maintain a neater and cleaner closet when you have only the amount you require? Are you glad that someone who has fewer clothes can now make use of yours? Why or why not? What do you think you received in this act of giving?

Keywords: Custodian, diminish

Affirmation: The more I give, the more I get.

49

Be kind, not self-righteous

"Be curious, not judgmental."
—WALT WHITMAN

Mercury and the Sculptor

Planet Mercury one day became curious about how worthy he was in the eyes of people on planet Earth. So he disguised himself as a man and went to a sculptor's studio. There were a number of beautiful, fascinating statues there. "How much does this cost?" asked Mercury, pointing to a statue of Jupiter. "That would be four coins," replied the sculptor. "Is that all?" responded Mercury, laughing. He next pointed to a statue of Juno and asked, "How much is that one?" "That is worth two coins," was the reply. "And how much for the one over there?" Mercury asked, pointing to a statue of himself. "Oh, I'll give you that for free, if you'll buy the other two," said the sculptor.

WoW: Imagine you're a brand-new parent. You love your baby. She can do absolutely anything, and you love her. She makes messes, makes loud noises, keeps you up at night, and you love her. Why is that? It's because it's you giving out the love—the baby can do no wrong. You already have this ability. There's nothing to learn. Why limit it to newborns or pets? You can do this with everyone you know. Sometimes a friend may say something mean, and you can love them; a loved one might do something that could hurt you, and you can love them. It's you. It's the Tao. Give out love no matter what. Miracles will show up around you.

Activity: Bring to share with your friends one dish that you absolutely love and one that you do not like very much. Notice how the foods that you consider yummy may not be preferred by some; likewise, the foods that you call "yucky" may be someone else's absolute favorite. Celebrate the differences.

Explore: Did you find it strange that not everybody likes or dislikes the same foods? Do you really think that some foods are tasty and some are yucky? Why is it that the foods that are yucky to you are tasty to another? Must people have similar tastes? In what other areas do you find such differences? Do you like being different?

Keywords: Notice, embrace

Affirmation: I accept you just as you are.

50

The immortal spirit enjoys a temporary human experience

> *"We are not human beings having a spiritual experience. We are spiritual beings having a human experience."*
>
> —Teilhard de Chardin

The Rose and the Amaranth

A rose and an amaranth blossomed side by side in a garden. The amaranth said to the rose, "You are so beautiful and smell so sweet; it's no wonder that you are a universal favorite." The rose replied, with sadness in her voice, "Ah, my dear friend, I bloom for a very short time; my petals soon wither and fall, and then I die. But your flowers never fade, even if they are cut. You are everlasting."

WoW: Picture a snake shedding its skin. Is it a new snake that remains? But it will shed its skin again and again. Is this a new snake that's left each time? Perhaps the snake never dies. Picture a caterpillar entering a cocoon and emerging as a butterfly. What happens to the caterpillar? Does it die? Each transforms, not dies. Imagine two caterpillars are walking along together, and a butterfly flies by overhead. One caterpillar (pointing to the butterfly) says to the other, "You'll never find me in one of those!" The caterpillar simply doesn't recognize his destiny and is therefore afraid of the unknown! We actually are immortal. Our bodies may wither, but you are not your body. Many people are afraid of dying, because they think it's unknown, but even that's not true. Before you were born into your current body, you were as "dead" as you will be after this life, and for as long a time, too! You don't have any bad memories of that time, do you? There's nothing to fear! Live without this fear.

Activity: Watch the video *Planetary Action Meditation: When Natural Disaster Strikes* on http://www.youtube.com or http://www.humanityhealing.net; then let an adult guide you through the meditation (within the same video) during which you may have the opportunity to experience your immortality and the immortality of Planet Earth. Experience the power of silent visualization.

Explore: How was the experience of silent visualization? When you sent healing and protection to Planet Earth, did you find yourself being protected too? Do you realize that you are a piece of God and the universe? If so, how?

Keywords: Infinite, secure, harmless

Affirmation: I am safe in the loving arms of my spirit.

51

The unseen power guides and protects without possessing

"Aerodynamically, the bumblebee shouldn't be able to fly, but the bumblebee doesn't know it so it goes on flying anyway."

—Mary Kay Ash

The Foolish Lion and the Clever Rabbit

Once upon a time, there lived a very ferocious lion in a forest. He used to kill many animals every day for no rhyme or reason. So all the animals got together and decided that each day, one animal would volunteer itself to be the lion's meal. One day, it was a rabbit's turn to go to the lion. This rabbit was old and wise. He took his own sweet time to walk to the lion's den. When the rabbit finally reached his destination, the lion was furious. The wise old rabbit stayed calm and said, "It's not my fault that I am late. A group of us rabbits were on our way to you when another lion attacked us and ate all my friends. I somehow escaped and managed to get here." The rabbit added, "The other lion was saying that he is the greatest." Hearing this, the lion was enraged and said, "Take me to that lion. I'll teach him a lesson." The wise rabbit agreed and led the lion to a deep well filled with water. The lion bent forward to take a look and started growling. Naturally, his image in the water—the other lion—also growled back at him. The lion jumped into the water to attack this other lion, only to be drowned in the well. To everyone's amazement, the rabbit, though small and insignificant, had discreetly saved the forest animals from the lion.

WoW: You were born as an empty slate—pure possibility, no great master plan for you from the Tao. You inherited traits from your parents, but that's not who you are. Sure, your parents raised you in certain ways, perhaps with a particular religion or belief system, with certain traditions, even eating certain foods and cultivating certain tastes, but that's not who you are. You start as nothing and take on what you wish, believe what you wish, become what you wish, and attract what you wish. Knowing this applies to you, you also know this applies to everyone else. You can see them that way: pure possibility, always having achieved what they took on for themselves. You can appreciate this in others. It is frequently hidden from them as well as from others around them, but you know!

Activity: Visit a farm or a zoo to witness the birth of a calf or other animal; or, alternatively, watch a video or movie showing the birthing process of any animal. Observe how the newborn has an inborn knowledge for surviving in this new environment, without receiving any training or guidance from outside.

Explore: Who do you suppose told the newborn what to do? Do you believe that you, too, have a similar guidance available to you? Have you experienced receiving guidance from an invisible source? When and how? Where do you think this source resides? Does everyone in the world have that guidance?

Keywords: Protection, divinity

Affirmation: I use my inner guidance for safety and protection.

52

All of creation can trace its origin to the same eternal mother

"We shall not cease from exploration, and the end of all our exploring will be to arrive where we began and know the place for the first time."

—T. S. Eliot

Androcles

A slave named Androcles once escaped from his master and fled to the forest. As he was wandering about, he found a lion lying down, moaning and groaning. At first he was frightened and turned to run away, but finding that the lion did not chase him, Androcles changed his mind and went up to him. As he came near, the lion put out his paw, which was all swollen and bleeding. Androcles found that a huge thorn had got into it and was causing all the pain. He pulled out the thorn and cleaned up the paw of the lion, which was soon able to rise and lick Androcles's hand like a dog. Then the lion took Androcles to his cave, and every day he would bring him meat so that he could survive. Shortly afterward, both were captured from the forest. Androcles was sentenced to be thrown to this lion, after the lion had been kept without food for several days. The Emperor and all his ministers came to see the show. Androcles was led out into the middle of the stadium. Soon the lion was let loose from his den. The lion rushed, roaring, toward his victim. But as soon as he came near Androcles, he recognized his friend and affectionately licked his hands. The Emperor was surprised, but when Androcles told him the whole story, he was deeply touched and freed his slave as well as the lion.

WoW: All things return to their source. The water in the oceans evaporates into the air and falls down again, returning to the ocean. Before the Big Bang, there was nothing. But this "nothing" turned out to be everything there ever was, packed down to a size smaller than the dot at the end of this sentence. And that nothing (or everything) exploded outward zillions of miles, only to find itself on a journey back (due to the universe's gravity) to nothingness, to be part of the next cycle of another Big Bang. Our scientists are discovering this as fact now. We are born from nothingness and will return to nothingness. We're all connected in this way. If you can see this in all things, from stars to grains of sand, from living beings to inanimate objects, you will discover a peace and a love worthy of discovering. We're all on the same journey—us and all things, big and small. Enjoy the ride.

Activity: Go outdoors and try to notice some of the smallest creations on our planet (tiny pebbles, small leaves, ants, bugs, etc.). Make a list of things you see. Enjoy the subtle but sure presence of these many tiny wonders. Next turn your attention to your own body. Notice how many billions of tiny cells make up your entire physical body. Give a silent gratitude to the mother of all creations.

Explore: Did you realize how often we miss witnessing the smallest creations on our planet? Why do you think this is so? Would you agree that the smallest in our world are equally important as the bigger creatures? Can you identify five small and five large creations that help humans (examples may include sand in sandpaper, bricks in buildings, etc.)?

Keywords: Brotherhood, intrinsic

Affirmation: Home is my favorite place in the world.

53

Honesty and compassion are divine qualities

"When I do good, I feel good; when I do bad, I feel bad. That's my religion."

—Abraham Lincoln

Water Goddess and the Lumberjack

A lumberjack was felling a tree on the bank of a river, when his axe flew out of his hands and fell into the water. As he stood by the water's edge, saddened by his loss, the water goddess appeared and asked him the reason for his grief. When the lumberjack told her why he was sad, she felt sorry for him and dived into the water and brought up a golden axe and asked him, "Is this the axe you had lost?" The lumberjack replied, "No, not this one." The Goddess then dived in a second time and brought up a silver axe and asked, "Is this the one you dropped?" "No, that is not mine either," said the lumberjack. She dived into the river once more and brought up the missing axe. The lumberjack was overjoyed at recovering his property, and thanked her warmly. The water Goddess was so pleased with the man's honesty that she presented him with the other two axes as well. When the lumberjack told this story to his friends, one of them felt very jealous and was determined to try his luck for himself. So he went and began to fell a tree at the edge of the river, and on purpose, dropped his axe into the water. The Goddess appeared as before, and on learning that his axe had fallen in, she dived and brought up a golden axe, as she had done on the previous occasion. Without waiting to be asked whether it was his or not, the fellow cried, "That's mine, that's mine," and stretched out his hand eagerly for the prize. However, the Goddess was so disgusted at his dishonesty that she not only declined to give him the golden axe but also refused to recover his own axe for him.

WoW: Do you notice how nice it feels when a friend shares a toy with you, or another person shares a piece of their cake with you? Sharing is the opposite of hoarding, yet so many people hoard. You see it in little children, saying "It's mine!" and they frequently fight. Imagine if the children were to say, "It's yours!" or "It's ours!" Fighting would instantly stop! There are many adults who haven't learned the wonderful feeling of sharing. Great wars are fought over "This land is my land," or "These riches are mine." Imagine if the leaders of the world were to say, "This land is yours; these riches are everyone's." Soon, all people would be sharing all things. Country borders would disappear. We would be one. The Tao is all about sharing, not hoarding; about giving, not only of things but of ourselves.

Activity: Organize a variety entertainment show (including skits, songs, dances, etc.) for some seniors at your nearest senior home community or old age home. Invite an adult to help you with the planning and other arrangements. Experience sharing your joy and compassion with these people, who may well remind you of your own grandparents!

Explore: Do you realize that you can make a big difference in someone's life? Did making others happy make you happy? Would you like for people to extend their compassion toward you and your family? In what other ways would you like to be of service to others?

Keywords: Equanimity, compassion

Affirmation: I always communicate with honesty and sincerity.

54

The power that creates the world is made visible in your good deeds

"If you want to lift yourself up, lift up someone else."
—Booker T. Washington

The Boy Bathing

A boy was bathing in a river one day; while splishing and splashing about, he moved a little too far away from the shore, into the deep water, and started crying, "Oh God save me!" A man passing by stopped when he heard the cries. He went to the riverside and began scolding the boy for being so careless as to get into the deep water, but then he finally saved him and brought him ashore. "Dear sir," said the boy, "I thought you might never help me, but now I see God in you and in your act of kindness."

WoW: You know the feeling you get when someone says something nice about you. You feel good, fill up with pride, and maybe take that good feeling and pass it along to another person, and that person passes on the good feeling to another. Did you ever imagine that this "wave" of your passing along a good feeling doesn't diminish—the wave you start (or one you're continuing) keeps moving from person to person, perhaps traveling around the world! You make a difference! The simple act of keeping alive a good feeling, or starting one, has an impact on others. Did you happen to see the inauguration of the President of the United States, Barack Obama, and the impact he had on others? Did you hear others say that now they will go make a difference? "They" are *you*. Your inspiration, your joy, is contagious. Who you are makes a difference.

Activity: Identify one person in your family or friends' circle who is feeling sad or had an accident and is in pain. Write them a note or copy a prayer and send it to them. Notice what a big difference it can make to their state of mind.

Explore: Was it difficult to make a difference in someone's life? Would you agree that the smallest acts of kindness can go a long way? Why or why not? To whom else can you send a loving note or render a kind gesture? In what ways would you like to receive kindness from others?

Keywords: Significance, blessed, magnificence

Affirmation: I make a positive difference with my thoughts, words, and actions.

55

Harmony and letting go endure, but not force and control

"Don't cry because it's over. Smile because it happened."

—Dr. Seuss

The Old Woman and the Wine Jar

Once there was an old woman who always loved a drink of wine. One day she spotted a wine jar lying in the road. She eagerly went and picked it up, hoping to find it full of wine. But when she picked it up, she found it completely empty. So the old woman held the jar up to her nose and took a long sniff of it and cried, "Ah, what memories cling to the objects of our desire!" She enjoyed the scent, even though there was no wine to drink.

WoW: Relax. Observe. Allow. These are the ways of being that make things flow easily. If you ever found yourself falling off the Eiffel Tower in Paris, you pretty much have two choices: scream and yell all the way down, or look at the surrounding scenery. Either way, you're going splat! Life is like that. Many people scream and yell through life, and not only do they have a difficult time, but they're unhappy. The way of the Tao is to look at the beauty and the scenery around you—that is, enjoy every moment without resistance. Without resistance you will be at ease, that is to say, with very little *dis*-ease—you'll experience life being much healthier, more energetic, and with a greater purpose. You will truly live. Nothing's wrong. Relax.

Activity: Spend an afternoon at an indoor play area like the "Gymboree," or outdoors at a play area in a park. Every time you begin to walk on a balancing beam, or climb a ladder or monkey bars (or for that matter, any equipment that calls for focus and caution), affirm, "With my luck, it is going to be easy." Observe how when you relax and let go—rather than focusing on "not falling" or "not losing balance"—you are able to do anything rather effortlessly.

Explore: How did it feel when you trusted your luck? Did it affect your performance or your experience at the play area? Do you know that you can be in harmony with your divine self? Do you believe there is an invisible power around you that always cooperates with you? Will you trust it and allow it to support you? If so, how?

Keywords: Unscathed, unimpeded, fortunate

Affirmation: I love and trust with total surrender.

56

You know best what to say and do

"Take the first step in faith. You don't have to see the whole staircase, just take the first step."

—Dr. Martin Luther King, Jr.

Belling the Cat

Long ago, a group of mice got together to discuss how they would outsmart their common enemy, the cat. Some said this and some said that; but at last a young mouse stood up and said, "You will all agree that our main danger is the tricky and sneaky manner in which the cat approaches us. Now if we could have some way of knowing that the cat is around the corner, then we would all be alerted and could hide." The young mouse continued, "Therefore, I suggest that we tie a bell around the cat's neck with a ribbon." Hearing this, an old mouse got up and said, "That's a great idea, but who will bell the cat?" The young mouse responded, "Have faith, we'll get the right idea at the right time."

WoW: Have you ever seen a great magic trick? Did you ask the magician how it's done? One of the reasons the magician doesn't tell is because after the telling, the "magic" is gone. Part of the excitement is the mystery. If you really want to, you can study magic on your own; and if you discover how it's done, then *you* have the magic. Life is like that. When you know something, you can keep the magic about it—the mystery about it—alive by simply *knowing*. Your life will be magical!

Activity: Get together with friends and choose some activities or play games where you communicate using only gestures. Have an adult support you in these activities. You may choose games such as Guesstures, Charades, Pictionary, and the like. Experience your connection with everyone in the room when no words are exchanged.

Explore: Did you enjoy this new way of communicating? Do you think it was effective? Were you able to understand your friends? How could you tell if your friends understood you? In what other situations can you be silent and yet be able to make someone understand you?

Keywords: Listen, settled

Affirmation: Being quiet and still allows me to hear my inner voice.

57

Do not impose rules

"You only have power over people so long as you don't take everything away from them. But when you've robbed a man of everything, he's no longer in your power - he's free again."

—ALEKSANDR I. SOLZHENITSYN

The Donkey and His Shadow

A traveler hired a donkey to carry him to a faraway place. The owner of the donkey also went along for a certain length of the journey. As the day was intensely hot, and the sun was shining in its full strength, the traveler stopped to rest and sought shelter from the heat in the donkey's shadow. There was space only for one person under the shadow of the animal, but the owner too wanted some space in the shade. A violent dispute arose between the two men as to which of them had the right to the shadow. The owner claimed that he had let only the donkey for hire, and not his shadow. The traveler asserted that he had, with the hire of the donkey, hired his shadow also. The quarrel proceeded from words to blows, and while the men fought, the donkey galloped off. Now neither the donkey nor his shadow could belong to either man.

WoW: What you resist, persists. That is, it stays around. If you push against a wall, it pushes back with the same energy, and nothing happens. If you leave the wall alone, it leaves you alone. Apply this to people, things, pain, desires, and leadership. When you let them all simply be (leave them alone), they will simply let you be. You will experience freedom from everything. When you're allowing everything to be, you're in a Tao space and at peace. If you apply authoritarianism, you will meet up with resistance. It must be so. True leadership is leadership by example, not by force or rules. You can be like this with your friends, and you will find that things go more smoothly.

Activity: Pair up with a friend, with whom there is a two- to three-year age gap between you. Invite an adult to facilitate this activity. The older child gets to be the "Big Brother" or "Big Sister" to the younger one, in that they are their mentor, coach, or leader for the duration of the activity. The older kids are to *allow* rather than interfere, and to lead by *demonstration* rather than force. Enjoy the dynamics of the teams and celebrate your successes and challenges along the way.

Explore: Was it easy being a big sister or big brother? If so, how? How was the experience of being led by your older friend? What did you like about this activity? What did you learn about yourself and your friend from this activity?

Keywords: Instinctive, sensible

Affirmation: My self-confidence allows me to be in charge of myself.

58

Life is a beautiful cycle of alternating good and bad fortunes

"Heaven on Earth is a choice you must make, not a place you must find."

—Dr. Wayne Dyer

The Hares and the Frogs

One day, all the hares gathered to cry about their unhappiness. They were all very scared because of the dangers on all sides from men, dogs, birds, and other beasts. So the hares decided that it would be better for them to die in peace than to live in fear; so they all rushed to a neighboring pool to dive in and drown. But on the bank of the pool, a large number of frogs jumped in fear upon hearing the sound that the hares were making. The frogs hid themselves in fear. Seeing all this, one of the wiser hares cried out, "Stop, friends, take heart; don't let us destroy ourselves. There are creatures in this world that are more timid than we are—they are afraid of us."

WoW: What is good or bad fortune? It is only a judgment, not an actual thing. Remove your judgments; they're not part of the Tao. But if you *do* judge, you might as well judge everything to be good! Remain untroubled in life! Look at these illustrations. The dot indicates where you are in life. In the first, it looks like you're at the top and having a wonderful time, but you're about to face a downward trend. Things look good now, but that will change very soon. In the second, life is pretty low, and you've been feeling bad, but things are about to look up. In the third, you're somewhere in the middle. Do you see how you can make up a lot of things about yourself? The truth is, you're in the fourth illustration, where you can truly create where you are in life – it's totally up to you! This *is* in fact where you really are!

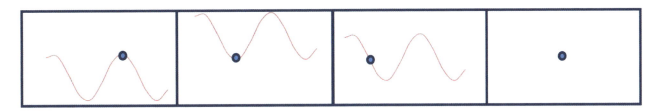

Activity: Devote a day to doing a variety of activities. You may invite an adult to assist you in choosing, planning, and organizing the activities. Make sure that the easy and not-so-easy activities interlace one another, so that you get a good taste of both experiences.

Explore: How was the overall experience? Which did you enjoy more, and why? Which did you not enjoy, and why? Can you see how "easy" and "tough" naturally come and go? Can you think of other times when you experienced both ease and challenge on the same day?

Keywords: Experience, movement

Affirmation: My life delights me with interesting challenges to help me grow.

59

Where there is moderation, there is no limit

"My limits will be better marked. Both the limits I will set, and my own limits."
—Isabelle Adjani

The Flies and the Honey Pot

One day a swarm of flies found a honey pot that had tipped over and had honey spilling out of it. The flies were overjoyed and decided not to leave the place until every single drop of honey was in their bellies. After a while, when they were ready to leave, they noticed honey sticking to their feet and wings, and they could not fly. "What stupid creatures we are! For a few hours of pleasure, we have risked our lives!" they cried. The flies felt regret for greedily consuming more than they required.

WoW: If you live from your heart, not from your thoughts, you will be surrounded by peace, softness, and grace. You will not need much, for who you are being is already fulfilled and nurtured—you have integrity. Integrity means being whole and complete—no parts missing. When there is integrity, there's no need to complete anything, for all is already complete. When things are complete, you don't *need* to accumulate anything. If you're not accumulating anything, you're living in moderation and with thrift. Without the *need*, there's the *freedom* to pursue anything, without limit. Now, nothing is impossible to achieve!

Activity: Observe a day of giving thanks where you present a handmade gift—made from recycled or biodegradable items—to a member of your family or a friend. Attach a note, stating why you are thankful to this person. Enjoy the feelings while creating this heartfelt, eco-friendly thank-you gift.

Explore: How was the experience of creating something precious for someone you love? Do you believe that a thank-you gesture must involve complex and fancy gifts? Why? Would it have been as special if you had gone to a store and bought a gift? Why or why not? Would you enjoy receiving similar thank-you notes and presents?

Keywords: Self-control, self-direction

Affirmation: I am without limitations.

60

Avoid harming another, and all of life's benefits will flow to you

"All that is necessary for evil to succeed is that good men do nothing."

—EDMUND BURKE

The Sheep and the Dog

A flock of sheep complained to the shepherd, "You treat us unfairly. We provide you with wool, lambs, and milk, but you give us nothing but grass—and even that we go out and graze ourselves. You get nothing at all from the dog, yet you feed him at your own table." The dog overheard this and said, "Please do not forget that if I was not here to watch over you, thieves would come in and steal you. You would be much too frightened to even graze." The sheep realized that whatever was happening was for their highest good, and they never again complained to their shepherd.

WoW: When you are centered—that is, when you know who you are, when you're at peace with the things around you—then even the *idea* of evil can't exist. There's no "evil" in nature, it's only in one's interpretation of events and circumstances; and that interpretation is up to you. If someone is behaving in a way that is commonly interpreted as evil, you can stay calm simply by knowing that this person forgot who he or she was and may be reacting to having a bad day, or even reacting to his or her interpretation that someone else did something evil to him or her! You can show compassion and understanding and not get caught up in furthering this way of being. When you are in the Tao space, you can always show this compassion to others, even if you don't know the circumstances.

Activity: Get together with your friends and, with the help of an adult facilitator, do any "White Light Protection" guided meditation (a suggestion: http://www.exploremeditation.com/meditation-video-white-light-protection/). This technique is believed to protect you from the influence of anyone or anything negative. Observe your feelings and state of mind.

Explore: Can you see how powerful you are? Are you more powerful than the so-called evils and dangers of this world? Why so? How would you use this power to benefit yourself and mankind in general? Can you sense God's protection over you?

Keywords: Sustainable, benevolent

Affirmation: I lend my support to every noble cause.

61

One wins friendship and trust by surrendering and remaining still

"You need not do anything. Remain sitting at your table and listen. You need not even listen, just wait. You need not even wait, just learn to be quiet, still and solitary. And the world will freely offer itself to you unmasked. It has no choice, it will roll in ecstasy at your feet."

—Franz Kafka

The Traveler and His Dog

A man and his dog were getting ready to begin a long journey together. The dog was stretching himself and relaxing on the couch by the door. Looking at the dog, the traveler said, "Come on; what are you waiting for? Hurry up now! Look how quickly I got ready. Get up, we have to leave soon." The dog merely wagged his tail and said, "I'm ready, master; it's you I'm waiting for."

WoW: One of the most powerful forces in the universe is gravity (it's the inherent power of "black holes"!). Gravity pulls things toward the lowest point. A river flows because it's seeking the lowest point. While it's flowing, it may be moving so swiftly that it forms whitecaps and turbulent currents. This swift-flowing water, when it reaches its goal, becomes so calm you can see your reflection in it! If *you* lay low, that is, if you stay quiet and calm, you will be the receiver of the natural goodness of the universe—things will flow to you naturally. It can't be any other way. If you try to force something to come to you, you will meet with resistance. This also can't be any other way. Stay low, stay calm, and stay at peace. You will be living the Tao.

Activity: Get together with friends to watch the documentary, "Ryan's Well." You may also visit the website http://www.ryanswell.ca for more information. This movie is about a young boy who has made an impact on humanity by using the least force and a lot of love. Be amazed at the power of least resistance and remaining under the radar.

Explore: Did the story touch and inspire you? Were you inspired to be like Ryan? In what ways can you be of service to someone? Is it easy to lay low and achieve great things? If so, how?

Keywords: Caring, camaraderie, maternal

Affirmation: I am naturally deserving of all the good in the world.

62

Forgive those who hurt you and accept everyone

"We make a living by what we get, but we make a life by what we give."
—WINSTON CHURCHILL

The Man and the Wooden God

In some cultures, people worshipped stones and idols to give them good luck and happiness. It happened that a man used to pray to a wooden idol he had received from his father. Although he prayed and prayed, each and every day, his luck did not seem to improve. He felt angry for receiving such a useless gift from his father and cursed his luck. After experiencing much frustration, the man one day decided to give the idol away to someone else; he didn't want anything to do with it anymore. So as the man was cleaning the idol and getting ready to wrap it up, it slipped and fell to the ground and broke in two; and guess what he saw? A large number of coins flying all over the place! The man had never realized that he had already been blessed with treasure for all those years. He had failed to see the gift, because he had neither appreciated it nor had the heart to share it with another. So, having learned his lesson, the man now took a large number of coins and distributed them to others in his community.

WoW: You were born as pure possibility. From that moment on, everything is an adventure, and everything shows up as a treasure and wonder to behold. Did you ever watch a three-year-old find a gorgeous flower in a field? It's pure joy and wonder. As people grow up, sometimes unfortunate things can happen; and sometimes their reaction to these things leaves them feeling sad and hurt, and perhaps angry. As they keep growing, they may try to get even with the universe by lashing out. These people are not evil; they simply forgot their ability to create joy and to connect to the divine. Perhaps they forgot their ability to forgive. *You* can help people return to themselves where their true satisfaction of being is—back to pure possibility, back to the adventure of life—by appreciating and loving them. This place is the treasure-house of the Tao.

Activity: Approach someone in your family or friends' circle that has said or done something that hurt you or disappointed you. Say to that person, "Who you *are* and what you *did* (or *said*) to me are separate things; and I still love you." Observe your emotions and their reaction to you.

Explore: How has your relationship with this person changed? Do you feel at ease with them now? If so, how? Would you be willing to accept an apology from someone? Do you believe that it is freeing when you do not associate someone with their actions? Why or why not?

Keywords: Kindness, depth

Affirmation: I have an abundance of love and joy to share.

63

Simplify the complicated

"Mishaps are like knives that either serve us or cut us, as we grasp them by the blade or the handle."

—JAMES RUSSELL LOWELL

The Crow and the Pitcher

A very thirsty crow found a pitcher with very little water in it. The crow tried drinking from it but found it impossible: her beak would not reach the water. She was dying of thirst. At last she hit upon a brilliant idea. She began dropping pebbles one by one into the pitcher; and with each pebble, the water rose a little higher, until at last it reached the brim. The crow could finally reach her beak into the water, and she drank to her heart's content.

WoW: When there's something we need to do, we usually look at the whole task and often feel overwhelmed. But in reality, once we get started, the "whole task" becomes the first task, and is always small and easy to do. Sometimes the idea of even the first task may feel overwhelming, but that's because you see the first task as also being a mini-project in itself! You can actually only do one thing at a time. Perhaps the first task starts with a phone call. That task is pressing a few buttons—pretty easy. In the moment of now, any task is trivial, because it actually takes no time! In successive moments of now, tasks get done effortlessly. Looking back on a completed task is often experienced as "Well, that was easy!" or "That wasn't so hard!" The difficulty of life lives only in your thoughts! And you can change your thinking! Go for it!

Activity: Choose a major project involving a week or two weeks' worth of effort (for example, doing fifty math problems, reading a one-hundred-page book, assembling a five-hundred-piece puzzle, etc.). With the assistance of an adult, enjoy planning the project and breaking it up into several small steps (solving five problems a day, reading ten pages a day, etc.). Be amazed at how such a major project was completed so easily by focusing on one step at a time and by keeping it small.

Explore: Do you think that there is any such thing as an impossible task? Did you find your experience with this project pleasant or tiresome? Why so? Do you believe that any difficult task can be made simple? Can you think of other areas in your life where you can simplify?

Keywords: Now, ease, sanity

Affirmation: Everything in my life is easy and manageable.

64

A journey of a thousand miles begins with one step

"Yesterday is history. Tomorrow is a mystery. And today? Today is a gift. That's why we call it the present."

—BABATUNDE OLATUNJI

The Hare and the Tortoise

A hare was once boasting about his speed to a group of animals. "I challenge anyone present to come and race with me," he said, "and I bet I can very easily defeat you." A tortoise said quietly, "I accept your challenge." "That is a good joke," said the hare. "I could dance around you all the way." "Do not boast until you've won," answered the tortoise. So a course was fixed, and the race started. The hare darted almost out of sight at once, but soon stopped and, believing that the tortoise could never catch up with him, lay down by the wayside to take a nap. The tortoise never stopped even for a moment and went on with a slow but steady pace, straight to the end of the course. When the hare woke up from his nap, he saw the tortoise just near the finish line. The hare ran as fast as he could, but it was too late. He saw the tortoise had reached the goal.

WoW: Notice the difference between these two ways of looking at running a race with a friend: in one way, you say "I'm going to win this race." In the other way you say, "I'm going to run as fast as I can and have fun." The first way involves an outcome; you may not win and may be disappointed. Also, the outcome is something in the future, not now. The second way has no outcome; it's something you say—it can't fail. It's a given that you'll have fun simply because you say so. When the race begins, the first way has some anxiety; the second is experienced in the now, and anxiety can't be present. What's the difference? In the now, total satisfaction exists. How can anything be wrong in the now? Each moment of now is perfect. All that exists is now, so there's no choice but perfection! Contentment, happiness, and peace all exist in the now. Be here, now.

Activity: Get together with friends and, with the help of an adult, identify a starting and a finishing point so that it takes approximately ten minutes to cover that distance by foot. Now begin your walk as a team. Focus on each step you take. Before you know it, you will have reached your destination. Celebrate how you completed the journey by beginning with the first step and then by taking *only* one step at a time.

For the second part of the activity, begin your walk back to the starting point by taking *longer* strides (the equivalent of two steps). Notice the difference.

Explore: Did you enjoy your walk? Which was easier, going or returning? Why do you think so? Where else in life can you apply this same principle?

Keywords: Potential, orderly, trivial

Affirmation: I focus easily and effortlessly, taking one step at a time.

65

Look within your heart for answers

"We cannot teach people anything; we can only help them discover it within themselves."

—GALILEO GALILEI

The Lion and the Dolphin

One day, while a lion was roaming by the seashore, he saw a dolphin lift up its head out of the waves. The lion said to the dolphin, "We have to be the best of friends, as I am the king of the beasts, and you are the king of the ocean." The dolphin gladly consented to this request. Not long afterward, the lion had a fight with a wild bull and called upon the dolphin to help him. The dolphin, though willing to assist him, was unable to do so, as he could by no means reach the land. The lion said, "You have turned out to be a traitor!" The dolphin replied, "No, my friend, please don't blame me. Nature has given me the power of the sea, but not the power of living on land."

WoW: When you try to force your ideas on others, you *must* run into resistance. It's the nature of things: when you push on something, it pushes back. It can be no other way. To avoid resistance, be simplehearted and *invite*—don't require. And know that to a true invitation, "No" is a legitimate answer. If you try to be clever and persuade someone to do something your way, you will probably encounter a clever response. If you know people are already whole and complete, you can simply share ideas with them and let them choose. There's harmony and love that way. You will be appreciated when you simply be yourself and allow others to be themselves. We don't really know what's best for others. They do.

Activity: Get together with friends to play a game based on questions and answers, such as Brainquest or Trivia. Invite an adult to ask you the questions. If you know the answer, raise your hand, but do not answer until the facilitator gives you the cue. Notice how you resist the urge to answer, or how you answer before the prompt, and also if you answer for another person in an attempt to correct or help them. Observe your mixed emotions and reactions in the process.

Explore: What did you enjoy most about this activity? What was the most challenging part? Why so? Do you believe that people have the ability to find answers for themselves? Do you believe that *you* have that ability?

Keywords: Egoless, innocence

Affirmation: I am more understanding and less demanding.

66

Humility is where real power lies

"If you would have a faithful servant, and one that you like, serve yourself."
—BENJAMIN FRANKLIN

The Rivers and the Sea

Once upon a time, all the rivers got together to complain at the sea for making their waters salty. "When we come to you," they said to the sea, "we are sweet and drinkable, but once we have mingled with you, our waters become salty and undrinkable." The sea responded, "Keep away from me, and you'll remain sweet." All the rivers wondered if this was even possible, and then they realized that they were naturally drawn to the calm sea.

WoW: Which are you drawn to more: a puppy that seems happy, or a snarling dog? Clearly, the happy puppy. The snarling dog, trying to get her way through intimidation and anger, winds up making others get out of her way. The puppy isn't trying anything—he's just being happy, but in so doing he attracts love and caresses! The calm sea is like the puppy: it invites others to come and play. You won't get what you think you want through force or demands. You will attract what you want by being humble and serving others.

Activity: Get together with friends. Each of you bring in a story of one of your real-life heroes—someone you are drawn to. Share with the group who this person is, what traits you like in him or her, and a real-life instance of how they exhibited humility. You may invite an adult to facilitate this process.

Explore: What did you learn from this activity? Do you feel energized and inspired? If yes, how? Were there any qualities that these "real-life heroes" had in common? Which ones?

Keywords: Natural, catalyst, cooperation

Affirmation: I join hands with you as your equal.

67

Lead with mercy, frugality, and humility

"The best index to a person's character is (a) how he treats people who can't do him any good, and (b) how he treats people who can't fight back."

—Abigail Van Buren

The Mean Fox and the Arrogant Stork

A fox invited a stork to dinner one day. The mean fox served his friend some soup on a flat plate. The fox could easily lap up the tasty soup, but the stork could not because of her long, pointy beak. The fox was amused at the scene, and the stork had to leave on an empty stomach. After a few days, the arrogant stork invited her friend the fox over for dinner. She served him some soup in a pitcher with a long, narrow neck. The stork could easily eat from the pitcher, whereas the fox was unable to even reach the soup. The stork finished her meal and said good-bye to the hungry fox.

WoW: You are in this adventure ride called *Life*. The ride existed before you were born, awaiting your arrival, and it will continue after your departure. Your journey is to enjoy the ride, not try to change the ride. How you can best enjoy the ride is to have mercy, be frugal, and be humble. That way your ego isn't interfering with your enjoyment of the ride. When you do not have mercy, your ego is present, and it ruins others' rides—and, therefore, yours as well. Similarly, to not be frugal or to not be humble brings the ego forth. The ego doesn't exist in the Tao—it interferes with the experience of being totally present, satisfied, and authentic. Enjoy the adventure!

Activity: With the help of some adults, organize a walk or road show to inspire people to live and lead with mercy, frugality, and humility. Enroll all age groups that believe in this philosophy. Observe how they automatically join hands with you and support this cause without any compulsion.

Explore: Did you enjoy the experience? How many came forward at the outset? How many new people joined you along the way? In what ways did this activity inspire you? Would you embody these qualities? How can you demonstrate this way of being in your own life?

Keywords: Detachment, dynamic, merciful

Affirmation: My potential and capacity to serve is divinely inspired.

68

Good friends work as a team instead of competing

"When love and skill work together, expect a masterpiece."

—JOHN RUSKIN

The Bundle of Sticks

An old man who was dying called his four sons to him to give them some parting advice. He asked his assistant to bring him a bundle of sticks and said to his eldest son, "Break it." The son tried and tried; he strained a lot, but was unable to break the bundle. The old man called all the other sons one by one to break the bundle, but none succeeded. "Untie the bundle," said the father, "and each of you take a stick." When they had done so, he said to them: "Now, break them," and each stick was easily broken. "You see my meaning," said their father. "You are strong when you are together and break easily when apart."

WoW: Have you noticed that the better you are at something, the more skilled you wish your opponent is? If you're a good tennis player, you don't enjoy playing against a beginner (unless you're teaching them!) as much as you do against someone of equal or higher skill, because that challenges you to play a better game yourself, and your skill is increased. Your opponent is really your partner, cooperating to help you improve. The same is true of anything you do—not just games or sports, but work and play too. When your partner, co-worker, playmate, opponent, or whoever is good at what they do, it naturally brings out the best in you. Seek people who help bring out your best simply by cooperation. Here's another example: first, imagine a drinking glass. No matter what liquid you pour into it, it takes the shape of the glass. They are 100 percent cooperating.

Activity: Get together with friends for a game such as volleyball, badminton, cricket, or any other sport where you play in teams. Before you begin playing, hang a tag or paste this message, "I support you," or "We are one team" onto each of your chests and backs. Observe how this reminder puts all players in a cooperative mood rather than one of competition.

Explore: Did it change the way you viewed your opponent in the game? Did you experience more love and cooperation toward the opposite team? Do you believe that your opponent also felt the same as you? Would you be able to hold the spirit of this message, even when the tag is absent? Why or why not?

Keywords: Collaboration, unity

Affirmation: I learn new, fun things with my team.

69

When hostility exists, there is no room for love

"Friendship with oneself is all important because without it one cannot be friends with anybody else in the world."

—Eleanor Roosevelt

The Horse and the Stag

A horse used to graze in a meadow, which he had all to himself. One day a stag came into the meadow and started grazing alongside the horse. The stag found some nicer, greener areas of the meadow for himself, and this irritated the horse a lot. So the horse decided to get the stag out of the meadow somehow. One day the horse saw a man visiting the area; and he approached him for help in getting the stag out. "Yes," said the man, "I will help you, but only if you allow me to ride you whenever I feel like it." The horse agreed to this, so the man put a bridle in the horse's mouth and a saddle on his back. The man and the horse together managed to drive the stag away from the pasture. But alas, due to his hostility towards the stag, the horse became the man's slave forever.

WoW: Imagine you were the only person in the entire universe. Aside from feeling bored, you would clearly long for someone else to be with you. Now imagine another person appears. Your entire existence and focus would be on the partnership and communication with this other being. You would share, laugh, cry, and be together. Who you are is *because* of this other being. Without her, you wouldn't share, laugh, communicate, interact, or even love. She is always your partner. Your being exists because of the contrast to her. You're alive. It's like there's no "in" without "out"—there's no "you" without "*not* you." This other being is not you! So now *you* exist! Now it so happens that there isn't only one other. There are over seven billion others, and they all help define you! How can any of them be your enemy? For one of them to be your enemy clearly requires you being your own enemy—it's in the definition of who you are! Don't see anyone as your enemy; see them as a *part* of who you are. This is the Tao.

Activity: Play "Tug of war" with a new set of rules. Hold the intention that the opposite team should not fall down or lose their balance. You may even rename this game "Tug of peace"! Observe how much useful energy is conserved with this intention. Now play the game in the manner it is normally played. Notice the difference in your energy levels.

Explore: Which version of the game tired you out the most? Why? Which game brought a sense of closeness with your friends on the opposite team? Did you enjoy the fact that neither you nor your friends on the opposite team lost the "Tug of peace"? How so? Can you still play the "Tug of war" for the sheer excitement of the game, rather than wanting to defeat the other team?

Keywords: Holiness, resolution, instrumental

Affirmation: I am grateful for the love I am giving and receiving.

70
Practicing the simplicities of life brings true joy

"The intuitive mind is a sacred gift and the rational mind is a faithful servant. We have created a society that honors the servant and has forgotten the gift."

—Albert Einstein

The Frog and the Ox

"Oh, Daddy," said a little frog to a big one sitting by a pool, "I saw such a terrible monster! It was as big as a mountain, with horns on its head and a long tail, and it had hoofs divided in two." "My child," said the old frog, "that was only Farmer White's ox. It isn't as big as you are describing; he may be a little bit taller than I, but I could easily make myself as broad as he; just you see." So he blew himself out, and blew himself out, and blew himself out. "Was he as big as that?" he asked. "Oh, much bigger than that," said the young frog. Again the old one blew himself out, and asked the young one if the ox was as big as that. "Bigger, Daddy, bigger," was the reply. So the frog took a deep breath, and blew and blew and blew, and swelled and swelled and swelled. And then he said: "I'm sure the ox is not as big as this!" But at that moment, he burst. The little frog cried, "Daddy, it was more fun when you were your normal, simple self!"

WoW: True satisfaction, happiness, and peace come from accepting things as they are. If you have a problem in life that you're trying to solve, try simply letting the problem be without solving it. It will disappear all by itself in a fairly short time. What keeps it going—what keeps it alive—is your trying to solve it! Look into your heart about the issue, not into your head, trying to figure it out and solving it. The universe doesn't require any solving. It doesn't pose questions that need answers. There is no need to understand everything, and the energy spent on getting the answers is better spent on peace and observing your surroundings without judgment. The universe doesn't depend on your understanding of it; it just *is*. It's best to simply observe and be excited at the privilege it is to witness the wonder. The path to peace, satisfaction and happiness is very easy to travel; all it takes is to stop thinking, analyzing, and figuring out what's right or wrong, or trying to get ahead. Peace, satisfaction, and happiness don't come from the intellect. Rather, they come from the source of who you are, from your heart. Just *be*. Soak it up—it's delicious! This is a God-realized life. This is the Tao.

Activity: Make a visit to a local monastery, convent, or spiritual retreat center. Dress up in your most ordinary, plain clothes, with no fancy accessories. Observe how everybody else dresses, what they eat, and how they treat each other.

Explore: How did you enjoy being in the company of the most simple of folks? Did you miss the fanfare, noise, and grandeur of places like malls, carnivals, and so forth? Why or why not? Is it easier to dress simply? Why do you think people like you or notice you? Is it because of the way you dress or for other reasons?

Keywords: Faith, simplicity, reverence

Affirmation: Every answer I seek resides inside me.

71

Awareness of the present moment removes all illnesses

"The basic thing is that everyone wants happiness, no one wants suffering. And happiness mainly comes from our own attitude, rather than from external factors. If your own mental attitude is correct, even if you remain in a hostile atmosphere, you feel happy."

—DALAI LAMA

The Walnut Tree

A walnut tree grew by the roadside and produced a large number of nuts each year. People who passed by wanted to pick walnuts from the tree, so they pelted its branches with sticks and stones to bring down the nuts. The tree felt a lot of pain and cried, "It is hard; the very person who enjoys the nuts I produce rewards me with sticks and stones." Hearing its cries, a passerby remarked, "There is no easier way to bring down your nuts other than using sticks and stones. So instead of being sad, why not consider that you are only serving others? Be appreciative of people who enjoy your walnuts; then your suffering will end."

WoW: Your body is a physical representation of what's going on in your mind. Anxiety can produce ulcers, for example. It has been shown that if you *think* you've been touched with a hot iron but were really touched with a pencil eraser, you could actually get a blister (Gordon L. Paul 1963)! To be physically healthy, all you need is to be mind-healthy—that is, be at peace, be happy. One way to be happy is to totally give up the idea that you need something to make you happy. Just be happy, right now. Nothing is lacking, nothing is needed; accept what *is* as perfection. Also give up the idea that this is difficult to do. After all, isn't it true that things are exactly as they are right now? That's called perfection. If your body is sick, then you realize that something you've been thinking or worrying about is attracting that sickness—perhaps you are denying some truth or are holding back some communication with somebody. When you tell the truth and communicate honestly, your bodily health will be more easily restored, because if your mind is pure, it will show up in your physical health.

Activity: Sit down with your friends in a circle. Let an adult facilitator invite each of you to quietly check in with yourself about where in your body you may be experiencing pain, tightness, or any other form of discomfort. Once each of you has identified the area and declared it to the group, say aloud together three times, "I am healed, whole, and complete—healthy me!" Then move onto playing or doing your favorite activity for about twenty minutes or so; then get together again in a circle to check in about how you feel.

Explore: What did you learn about yourself from this activity? Did it seem magical that when you were engaged in your favorite activity, you hardly noticed the discomfort? Why do you suppose this happened? Do you believe that a healthy mind is responsible for a healthy body? Will you always think positive and loving thoughts? If so, how?

Keywords: Centered, choice, happiness

Affirmation: I say "yes" to now.

72

Admire and accept the perfect miracle that is you

"People usually consider walking on water or in thin air a miracle. But I think the real miracle is not to walk either on water or in thin air, but to walk on Earth. Every day we are engaged in a miracle which we don't even recognize: a blue sky, white clouds, green leaves, the black, curious eyes of a child—our own two eyes. All is a miracle."

—Thich Nhat Hanh

The Stag at the Pool

A thirsty stag went to a pool to drink some water. As he bent down to quench his thirst, he noticed his own reflection in the water. He was struck with admiration for his beautiful antlers, but at the same time felt disgusted, looking at his slender legs. While he was appreciating himself, a lion attacked him. The stag ran as fast as he could and got out of the lion's sight, but then his antlers got caught in some branches. He was unable to free himself in time and thus fell prey to the lion. "Woe is me!" cried the stag, "I looked down upon my legs, which might have helped save my life, but I glorified my antlers, which have got me into trouble today."

WoW: Picture a small child seeing a beautiful flower or a grasshopper for the first time. Imagine an adult seeing her first shooting star, or being on an airplane for the first time. All these experiences and thousands more have an "awe-quality" to them. It's inspiring, exciting, invigorating! This comes partly from the newness of the experience. What you may not know is that you have the ability to give each experience this new quality! After all, isn't every moment a new moment that never was before? We often get into the habit of comparing this moment with past moments, and that connection makes this moment seem not new. You can break than connection by accepting yourself and your circumstances totally in the now, and hence experience the wonder of life.

Activity: Observe some of the wondrous yet undervalued creations (such as a bird's nest, a spider's web, an anthill, your own pet, etc.). Notice how carefully, skillfully, and artistically these creatures in nature have created their homes or are going about following the guidance of their innate nature.

Explore: Were you impressed with what you witnessed? What struck you the most? Could you weave a nest or a web with as much skill as the creatures themselves?

What makes these creations so special? Have you ever stopped before to admire these small wonders of our planet? Would you now pay attention? What insignificant aspects of yourself will you now focus upon?

Keywords: Awareness, curiosity, miraculous

Affirmation: Thank you God for filling my days with miracles.

73

Live in grace, and trust that prayers are answered in perfect time

"I think we all have a little voice inside us that will guide us. It may be God, I don't know. But I think that if we shut out all the noise and clutter from our lives and listen to that voice, it will tell us the right thing to do."

—Christopher Reeve

The Bat and the Weasels

A bat fell to the ground one fine morning and was captured by a weasel. The bat begged the weasel not to kill him. "Alas," said the weasel, "I cannot let you go, because the weasel is the enemy of all birds." "But I'm not a bird, I'm a mouse!" exclaimed the bat. "Ah, I see that you are a mouse," said the weasel, "only when I look at you closely." The weasel let him go. Sometime afterward, the bat was again caught by another weasel. The bat again begged this weasel to let him go. "No," said this weasel, "I have never ever let a mouse go." "But I'm not a mouse," said the bat, "I'm a bird." "Well, so you are," replied the weasel, and set the bat free. Thus, the bat managed to escape the weasels, no matter what the situation.

WoW: There's a natural flow to the universe. As long as you go with the flow, things will happen naturally and peacefully. If you resist the flow, you will encounter turbulent times. The flow has a rhythm and a pace. If you try to change the natural rhythm of that flow, you will be less effective. For example, if you foolishly try to make tomorrow arrive sooner, you will meet up with failure and frustration! From a dog's point of view, he's never late. He's always exactly on time! When you create the experience that everything is happening exactly as it should, your actions are considered bold, because many others are not having this experience. Things do happen as they do, don't they? Your choices are to accept this or reject this, but neither changes the facts. There's real power in accepting the flow of the Tao.

Activity: Devote a day to doing everything you normally do, only more slowly and consciously. Get together with your friends and, in the presence of an adult, eat your snack or meal without talking, very slowly and mindfully; walk instead of run; and play your favorite games, mindfully. Try doing everything in slow motion. Observe how your body and mind feel at the end of the day. Get together with your group and share your experience.

Explore: How did your body feel? How did your mind feel? Did you have more energy than yesterday? Did you like the taste of your food better? Do you feel more relaxed and peaceful? Why or why not?

Keywords: Respectful, cautious, active

Affirmation: I acknowledge that every moment of my life is a blessing and an opportunity.

74
All things here today are gone tomorrow

"Seeing death as the end of life is like seeing the horizon as the end of the ocean."

—DAVID SEARLS

The Old Man and Death

An old laborer was busily gathering sticks in a forest. At last he grew so tired and hopeless that he threw down the bundle of sticks and cried out, "I cannot bear this life any longer. I wish death would only come and take me!" As he spoke, Death appeared and said to him: "What's the matter? I heard you calling me." The old man was taken aback, for he did not expect to see Death appear before him. "Please, sir," replied the old man, "would you kindly help me lift this bundle of sticks onto my shoulder?" The old man realized in time that his feelings of frustration and hopelessness needed to die, not his body!

WoW: Imagine yourself tomorrow. Imagine yourself one thousand years from now. Imagine yourself yesterday. Imagine yourself one hundred years ago. Is there much of a difference? Do you see you can place yourself anywhere and at any time? All there is, is this present moment, now, yet you can put yourself anywhere. This is always true. For billions of years, before you were born into this lifetime, where were you? You were dead, or not yet alive; you were in formation. That wasn't bad, was it? There was nothing to fear. The same is true for the next several billion years. There's nothing to fear! You've been there already, and look at you now! The fear of death can only exist when you are not living in the now. Be here now, and death dies.

Activity: Watch a video on http://teacher.scholastic.com/activities/studyjams/water_cycle/ or arrange a fun presentation by an adult on the subject of the water cycle, where water evaporates, forms a cloud, falls as rain, and the process repeats. Observe and discuss how only the form changes, but the essence that makes up this phenomenon does not go away. Also discuss among yourselves the parallel topic of human life and death cycles.

Explore: What do you think about these phenomena that have been going on for ages? Can you see how humans and animals experience cyclical changes, just like the environment? Has anyone (person or pet) you've known passed away recently? Can you now believe that they may be living in a different form? Why or why not?

Keywords: Formless, ethereal, alchemy

Affirmation: I greet each day refreshed and renewed.

75

Place fewer demands on yourself and others

"There are only two lasting bequests we can hope to give our children. One of these is roots, the other, wings."

—Hodding Carter

The Tortoise and the Eagle

A tortoise was frustrated with being confined to the ground and wanted to be able to fly high up in the air with the birds. So he went up to an eagle and said, "Will you please teach me how to fly?" "It is of no use," replied the eagle. "You are not meant to fly. Your place is on the ground. Just be yourself." The tortoise refused to listen and continued to beg, "Please, please don't say no, Mr. Eagle; teach me the tricks of the air." Eventually, the eagle grew tired of arguing with him. He picked him up in his claws, soared high up in the air, and said, "Now fly," and then let him go. The tortoise landed on a huge rock and was dashed to pieces.

WoW: If you had a small flowerpot and tried to grow fifty flowers in it, they would wither and die. If you grew one or two flowers in it, they'd flourish. Giving things and people the room to grow on their own enables them to flourish. If you say to your friends, "Don't do this" and "Don't do that," they'll soon stop being your friends! If you tell them to do what they want, or ask them what they'd like to do, they have room to be and to express themselves and will be your friends for a long time! Celebrate your ability to allow others to be themselves, and they'll allow you to be yourself. Life is for celebrating!

Activity: Play with building blocks (LEGOs or any other kind) by randomly pulling out one block at a time and creating whatever you feel like in that instant. Do not plan ahead what to make. See what wonderful creations come forth as a result of placing fewer demands on the final result. Enjoy the experience of creating random designs, each a masterpiece in itself.

Explore: How was this experience of creating random designs? Was it fun to anticipate what might be the final looks of your creation? Do you think it is nice to sometimes rest easy and let the moment tell you what to do? Why or why not?

Keywords: Autonomy, exemplify, encourage

Affirmation: I always have ready access to whatever I need

76
True power lies in being flexible at all times

"I am a man of fixed and unbending principles, the first of which is to be flexible at all times."

—Everett Dirksen

The Oak and the Reeds

An oak tree, growing on the bank of a river, was uprooted by a severe gust of wind and thrown across the stream. It fell among some reeds that were growing by the water and said to them, "How is it that you, who are so delicate and slender, were able to withstand the strong winds, whereas I, who am stronger have been uprooted and thrown across the river?" "You were stubborn," came the reply, "and fought against the storm: but we bowed and yielded to the wind, and so the storm passed over our heads without harming us."

WoW: Do you know how bullfighters fight bulls? They use space to take the energy of the bull. In that space, the energy disappears. There's actually a type of martial arts called "Aikido," which is based on this principle. Imagine a bullfighter standing firm in the path of the bull—he would be severely injured. The bending gives him his strength. If you are soft and flexible in life, you will find that life flows easily through you. If you are resistant to what is, life will be hard. Being soft and flexible also includes your thoughts. Holding on to what you believe as being right is not being flexible, and simply maintaining your rightness will be unsatisfying. It's fine to have an opinion about things, but allowing room for others' opinions allows you to have a more flexible and satisfying life.

Activity: Get together with your friends and, with the help of an adult, lay out various kinds of obstacle courses in a park or in someone's backyard. Now pretend to be a "strong tree." While pretending to be the "strong tree," try going through the obstacle courses. Observe how the "strong tree" will not be able to go through intricate obstacle courses without changing its shape/stance and bending (or being flexible).

Explore: Has your concept of strength altered? Which has the ability to course through the obstacles—the "strong tree" or the "flexible reed"? Can this idea apply to how you live your life, too? Can you suggest some areas where bending and being flexible is more effective than being rigid and strong? Why so?

Keywords: Yielding, tenderness

Affirmation: My open, flexible nature draws people to me.

77
Abundance grows when excess is given away

"Everything in excess is opposed to nature."

—HIPPOCRATES

The Brother and Sister

Once there was a man who had two children, a son and a daughter. Many considered the boy to be good-looking, but not the girl. One day the two were playing inside the house, and the brother happened to pass by a mirror on the wall. He stood still in front of the mirror and boastfully remarked to his sister, "Look how handsome I am!" The girl felt sad and ran to her father and complained, "Brother is so arrogant; he hurt my feelings." The father called both his children to him and embraced them both very lovingly. He then turned first to his son and said, "If you think you have an abundance of good looks, then why spoil it with behavior like that? Drop your arrogance, and watch your looks enhance." The father next turned to his daughter and said, "If you think that you are lacking in good looks, why not counter that with your abundant wisdom and understanding? Let go of your desire for good looks, and watch your inner beauty enhance."

WoW: When you feel happy and excited about something, do you notice that one of the most important things is that you share it with others? You can't keep it to yourself. And when you *do* share it, your excitement grows; it doesn't shrink. This is a natural way of the universe. When you have a lot, you give it away. When you have a little, you seek others to help fill the empty feeling. Now imagine that you're sad or angry. You can share that with the universe, and it will return healing. This way of being is actually Tao-like, and to do otherwise leaves you not feeling as peaceful and satisfied. Imagine being selfish with your joy and not sharing it! That is hard to do, and even if you can, you're robbing others of an opportunity to receive your energy. If you want to live a life of joy and fulfillment, be Tao-like. Be willing to discover that the more you have, the better it is to give it away or share it.

Activity: Starting today, for the next twenty-one days, collect one item of yours every day and put it in a hamper or box. Look for things that you have in excess, or whatever else you feel like, but remember that they must be donated. Observe how light and fulfilled you feel after this exercise.

Explore: Were you glad that you shared your surplus belongings with others? Do you feel less cluttered with stuff around your house or room? Do you believe that your gesture might have benefited many others? If so, how? Are you inspired to regularly offer excess stuff that collects in your house to others? Why?

Keywords: Balance, circulation, constructive

Affirmation: I feel abundant every time I share a smile or a treat.

78

The soft and supple is often stronger than the rigid and hard

"Nothing is so strong as gentleness, and nothing is so gentle as true strength."

—Ralph Sockman

The Ant and the Dove

An ant stood by a river to quench his thirst, but while drinking, he tumbled in and almost drowned. A dove, sitting on a nearby tree, saw the ant in danger, quickly plucked a leaf, and dropped it into the water so that the ant could climb onto it and be carried to safety. A little later, a hunter arrived there and was just about to cast his net over the dove. The ant saw this and quickly bit the hunter's leg. The hunter was distracted and dropped the net just in time for the dove to fly to safety.

WoW: Have you ever heard that you are about 60 to 75 percent water? Do you know that water covers about 70 percent of the surface of the Earth? Scientists who are looking for life on other planets start by looking for the existence of water or ice. Water is life. Water flows smoothly and has no sharp edges. Flowing water, though soft, eventually wears away the hardest things, yet it remains soft. That's how the Grand Canyon was formed! It's a great model for your life—be like water: stay soft, stay flowing. Nothing will harm you; you will harm nothing. You will simply be on the joyous ride of life, sometimes fast, sometimes slow, but smooth and exhilarating. Your strength is in your softness.

Activity: Conduct an experiment in which you take a long, unbreakable, transparent container. Fill up the container with pebbles, shells, beads, sand, and so on. Make sure that the container is completely filled up and there is no room for any more articles. Now observe what happens when you pour water into the container—see how water finds the seemingly insignificant areas to go and settle. There is always room for water, as it is soft and changeable.

Explore: What did you learn from this experiment? Who would you rather be like, the hard stones or the soft water? Why so? Can you find other areas in your life where you can be like water?

Keywords: Fluid, willing

Affirmation: Compassion and softness make me strong.

79

Where there is harshness, extend kindness

"There is no revenge so complete as forgiveness."

—JOSH BILLINGS

The Four Oxen and the Lion

A lion used to prowl about a field in which four oxen lived. Often he tried to attack them, but whenever he came near, they turned their tails to one another, so that whichever direction he approached them from, he was met by the horns of one of them. One day, for some reason or other, the oxen started quarrelling among themselves, and each went off to graze alone in separate corners of the field. Then the lion attacked them one by one and had soon killed all four. Had the oxen resolved their differences amicably, they might have still kept the lion at bay and be grazing together, merrily.

WoW: As human beings, we want to be right, but that desire is at the heart of all resentments and fighting. Even if you are right, and even if you win an argument, what you're left with is not a feeling of love and closeness. Which would you rather be: right, with a feeling of tension, or happy, with a feeling of love and connection? It seems pretty obvious which is a more satisfying way of being, yet it often seems so difficult to give up being right. It takes practice. It takes acceptance of another's point of view. Accepting it doesn't mean you have to agree with it, but it does mean letting go of your insistence on being right. What makes it so hard is that we mistakenly think our opinions define us, but they do not—they're just opinions. With practice it becomes easier, and you'll very quickly see the benefit. It also keeps you physically healthier—and certainly more Tao-like. Give up being right.

Activity: Conduct this experiment (inspired by a video on www.youtube.com) in which you pour about half a cup of some brightly colored juice (such as cranberry, pomegranate, or grape) into a large bowl. The juice represents resentment or negative thoughts, and the bowl represents our mind. In order to nullify the effects of negative energy, you start pouring water, which represents love or positive thoughts, into this bowl in very small quantities (say, half a cup) at a time. As you continue pouring water into the bowl, the color of the juice starts getting lighter and lighter, until eventually it becomes colorless, just like water. This represents how positive thoughts can nullify negative thoughts.

Explore: Which do you suppose is more powerful, resentment or love? What kind of person would you rather be, resentful or loving? In what areas of your life can you be more forgiving? How would you go about it?

Keywords: Goodwill, giving, initiative

Affirmation: I am forgiving.

80

Paradise is appreciating life in the here and now

"Appreciation is the highest form of prayer, for it acknowledges the presence of good wherever you shine the light of your thankful thoughts."

—Alan Cohen

The Peacock and Juno

The peacock was unhappy because he did not have a beautiful voice like other birds, so he complained to Goddess Juno about it. He said, "All the birds envy the nightingale's beautiful singing voice; but when I utter a sound, everyone laughs at me." The goddess answered him, "You have so much beauty; your neck flashes like emeralds, and your tail is full of gorgeous color." The peacock was still unhappy, and said, "What is the use of such beauty with a voice like mine?" Juno replied, "Nature has given every creature its own unique gift: to you beauty, to the eagle strength, to the nightingale voice, and so on; you alone do not see the obvious." The peacock felt wonderful hearing this and felt happy for his gifts.

WoW: When you were born, you had all your needs supplied by the love of your family. When you were a toddler, you were happy simply being with your family. The happiest times are spent simply doing anything with those you love. As you get older, your "family" expands to include friends, and then the happiest times are with family and friends. What all these fun times have in common is *you*! You are your best friend and closest family, and that stays with you forever. There's no need to look outside yourself for happiness, when happiness comes from inside you. You should realize you don't do things or go places to be happy; you bring your already existing happiness wherever you go. As long as you realize this, you'll be content whatever you do and wherever you go, because you always have your closest friend and family (which is *you*) with you and need nothing! Go play!

Activity: Make a list of people and things in your life that you often take for granted (example: parents, food, pet, toys, etc.). Write a prayer or note of appreciation to them. Observe how happy, fulfilling, and freeing this experience can be for you.

Explore: Did you find it easy or difficult to identify people and things to appreciate in your life? Have you been appreciated by others? Do you like being appreciated for who you are? In what other ways can you appreciate yourself and others?

Keywords: Bestow, appreciate

Affirmation: "Thank you" is my favorite prayer.

81

Be good, do good; and give more, hoard less

"No one has ever become poor by giving."

—Anne Frank

The Flea and the Ox

A flea once said to an ox, "How come a big, strong fellow like you is content doing all the hard work for people, while I, who am so tiny, live on their bodies and drink their blood without having to do any work at all?" The ox replied, "Men are very kind to me, and so I am grateful to them; they feed me, give me a place to stay, and, every now and then, show their affection by patting me on the head and neck." "If I gave more and took less, they would pat me too," remarked the flea.

WoW: If you want something, then not having it brings up a feeling of lack and dissatisfaction until you get it (if you do), but then you want the next thing and the next, and you have a life full of things you lack! On the other hand, if you want nothing, that's simple to acquire! You *have* nothing, which is to say you are instantly fulfilled! That may sound silly, but it's absolutely true, because if you want nothing, you lack nothing. This means you're totally satisfied with what you have, and that's the secret of happiness! Just as you can't have hot without cold, you can't have *nothing* without also having *everything*! You go around life being fulfilled and satisfied. Then you remain satisfied with whatever "somethings" you get—whatever life hands you. It's wonderful. May you always have nothing!

Activity: Play the game, "Where did it come from?" Choose one item at a time, and try to trace its origin. For instance, your friend could hold up a banana and ask, "Where did the banana come from?" You may say, "From the store." Then the friend asks where the store got it; you may say, "From the farm," and so on, until you find that you trace its origin to nothing! You may also use items such as paper currency, clothes, and so on. Now with the help of an adult facilitator, discuss why accumulating too much of anything (including the items used in this game) may be unnecessary if you can manifest anything you desire from the invisible (nothing)!

Explore: Is it possible that everything you observe around you came from nothing? What do you believe will happen once the item gets old, decays, or dies? Can you trace its path and final destination? Can you imagine where *you* must have come from? Do you acknowledge that you have creative powers within you? How differently do you view the idea of accumulation?

Keywords: Nothingness, creativity

Affirmation: I have the ability to create anything from nothing, and I see no value in hoarding.

References

"A Few Favorite of Aesop's Fables." *http://bygosh.com/*. http://bygosh.com/aesop/index.htm.

Aesop's Fables: Planet PDF e-book

"BrainyQuote." *BrainyQuote*. http://www.brainyquote.com/.

"Contentment." *Proverbia.net*. http://en.proverbia.net/citastema.asp?tematica=247&page=1

Dyer, Wayne. *Change Your Thoughts-Change Your Life: Living the Wisdom of the Tao*. Carlsbad, CA: Hay House, Inc, 2007.

Dyer, Wayne. *Living the Wisdom of the Tao: The Complete Tao Te Ching And Affirmations*." Carlsbad, CA: Hay House, Inc, 2008.

Favorite Fables In Prose and Verse: London, UK: Griffith and Farran.

Fox, Erol. "Inherent Excellence BLOG." *http://inherentexcellence.com/blog/*. March 15, 2010. http://inherentexcellence.com/blog/?p=345

"Hercules and Pallas." *http://www.aesopfables.com/*. http://www.aesopfables.com/cgi/aesop1.cgi?srch&fabl/HerculesandPallas.

"Hippocrates Excess Quotes & Sayings." *searchQuotes*. http://www.searchquotes.com/Hippocrates_/Excess/quotes/

"Inspiring Potential Quotes." *Manifestyourpotential.com*. http://www.manifestyourpotential.com/life/game_of_life/discover_your_potential/quotes_personal_potential_famous_inspirational.htm

"Phrases from Shakespeare." *The Phrase Finder*. http://www.phrases.org.uk/meanings/phrases-sayings-shakespeare.html

"Quotes About Letting Go." *Goodreads*. http://www.goodreads.com/quotes/tag/letting-go

"QuoteWorld: Forgiveness." *QuoteWorld.org*. http://www.quoteworld.org/categories/forgiveness/

"Stillness and Inspirational Quotes." *Be Still Now*. http://www.bestillnow.com/Quotes.htm#Stillness_Quotes

"Thinkexist.com." *thinkexist.com*. http://thinkexist.com/quotations.

"Top 20 Letting Go Quotes." *EdwardKhoo.com*. http://edwardkhoo.com/top-20-letting-go-quotes/

"Wisdom Quotes – Quotations to challenge and inspire." *Wisdom Quotes*. http://www.wisdomquotes.com/

About the Authors

Nilanjana lives a life that is an expression and reflection of her life's purpose, which is being the change she wants to see in her children, through living a life in harmony with nature. As an advocate for children—who are the future and hope of our planet—she invites all individuals, families, and institutions that influence our children to join hands in becoming the change first. She extends this way of being to all facets of her life, from choosing the right foods to patronizing eco-friendly and conscious companies that are aware of their impact on our world. Nilanjana firmly believes that the choices we make in each moment will determine the future we create and bestow on our future generations. She holds a bachelor's degree in engineering and a master's degree in business administration and has worked in engineering and information technology industries in sales and business development. She is a volunteer with the Distance Healing Network as a Reiki Level 2 healer. Nilanjana lives in Seattle, WA, with her husband Venkatesh and their two lovely boys, Harsha, eight years old, and Rishab, three years old.

Bob contributes his vision of self to people of every generation. He uses his self-expressions of humor, irony, silliness, intelligence, beauty, vulnerability, lightness, joyfulness, and compassion to make a difference in the lives of others by standing for their personal transformation. His inherent talent for taking life "lightly" and not focusing too much on the "stuff" of life, combined with his grace for living, translates his vision into something tangible, making a positive difference in people's lives. Bob holds a bachelor's degree in mathematics. He is a Microsoft Excel MVP (Most Valuable Professional) and an employee of KPMG in New Jersey, USA. He has authored two books: *This Isn't Excel, It's Magic!* and *Excel Outside the Box*. Bob lives in Palisades, NY, with his wife Judy. They have two beautiful children—Stefanie, twenty-nine years old, and Jared, twenty-one years old—and a precious granddaughter, Lilith, who was born on Bob's birthday!

Dhivya is an embodiment of creative expression. The purity and innocence of her heart are reflected in all of her interactions, including her sketches and drawings. She holds a bachelor's degree in engineering and a master's degree in information systems and works as a senior software engineer for Fidelity Investments in India. Dhivya celebrated her first wedding anniversary with Charles Prabhu in February 2013!

Made in the USA
Charleston, SC
31 May 2013